Tales from La Perla

A Misspent Hippie Youth

Ralph M. Flores

TALES FROM LA PERLA
Copyright 2018 by Geri M. Rhodes
Second edition 2021
Tome Lane Books

All rights reserved. No part of this book may be reproduced or transmitted in any form or by any means without written permission from the Copyright holder.

ISBN 978-1-7328852-1-9

Front cover photograph courtesy of Bob Christensen

Back cover photographs: left, courtesy of Barbara Muller right, Photo by Geri Rhodes

Title page photograph courtesy of Gary Hutchinson

To our children, Gabe, Elena, and Adam

and their families

and to Ralph's friends who helped realize this book:

Alex, Betty, BG, Bob, Hank, Laura, Leo, and Richard

In a story, fact and fiction become one.

"My Life and the Existential Duck Pop"

Ralph M. Flores   Photo courtesy of Bob Christensen

Contents

- 7 Photographs
- 8 Foreword by Geri Rhodes
- 10 Introduction by Leo Bottos
- 11 Beely and Me
- 15 La Perla
- 23 La Perla People
- 28 TV in La Perla
- 30 Sex and the Single Male
- 35 Homecoming
- 53 Homebuilding
- 57 Good Dog
- 62 Confrontation
- 70 Homebuilding II
- 73 Working on the Well
- 81 A Death
- 86 Babe
- 90 Weeds
- 97 Bindweed and Me
- 98 Spence
- 103 La Perla Spring
- 109 The Eyes of Jesus
- 115 Showers
- 119 In Praise of Eve
- 122 Shane Revisited
- 133 Industry
- 139 Voices
- 143 A Birth
- 148 Commitment
- 155 Law West of the Rio Grande
- 161 Feast!

Beyond La Perla

171 Beyond La Perla
172 My Life and the Existential Duck Pop
181 Hitchhiking
194 Two People on a Journey by Alex Sanchez
195 Bulletin Board
200 We Actually Called Him Raf by Betty Mishuk
202 Firewood Run
207 The Iliad at 4 a.m.
208 Lunch beneath the Bo Tree
214 Rocks
218 Afterword by B.G. Burr

Photographs

1. Ken Hansen's house (Front cover)
2. Rio Grande Pueblo petroglyph, Tomé Hill (1)
3. Ralph (Frontispiece 4)
4. Highway's end (14)
5. Post Office (22)
6. Louie's house (52)
7. Roof with stove pipe (72)
8. Ladron at sunset (108)
9. House with hour glass I (154)
10. House with hour glass II (160)
11. The Great Majestic (171)
12. T.G. Scott (206)
13. Old adobe under trees (213)
14. Carlo's Rock (217)
15. Raf at B.G.'s (219)

Foreword

I always liked these stories, so when others asked to read them, I put *Tales from La Perla* at the front of the line of manuscripts Ralph left behind—among them a post-apocalyptic novel, fables and moral tales, and many poems. Ralph had listed a partial table of contents on a small note pad, and there was a folder labeled "*La Perla* tales to organize." I think he never got around to integrating the two and have puzzled about why. Were they too personal? Might some people recognize themselves and feel hurt at the portrayal? Might they say, that's not the way it was, not that way at all? He would have said, "It's fiction."

About a week after Ralph died in June 2017, I found his backup flash drive on the ground in our yard near my car. I don't know how it got there, but I took it as a sign and a permission. It's now more than a year later, and I've found the process of putting the stories together painful but comforting. Reading Ralph's work now that he's gone is very different from reading it while he was alive. I can't consult him or watch his reaction to what I say.

So be it.

I knew Ralph when he was at mile marker zero in the town he calls La Perla, knew him before and for many years after. We were married for nearly thirty-seven years up to his death. I knew many of the people he gave pseudonyms, and most to me are recognizable, so I'm guessing others will find them so as well. I thank Leo, many miles away, for writing the Introduction; BG for writing the Afterword and for his help preparing the manuscript for printing; Hank and Bob for returning to La Perla with me; Bob for his impeccable black and white photos and Betty and B.G. for theirs; Betty, Laura, and Richard for their tributes; Alex for his memory of how he met Ralph and Jon; and Ken, who, the day before he died, gave me the red depression-glass artifact Ralph would have added to his wall had he found it at the time. Leo told me he didn't realize how much living in La Perla meant to Ralph before he moved on to Edge City. All told, Ralph stayed in La Perla close to five years, but what he learned lasted a lifetime.

Geri Rhodes aka Jeni
Tomé, New Mexico

Introduction

I first met Ralph soon after my arrival in New Mexico while he was teaching a Chicano literature course at the University of New Mexico. Friends of mine, ex-servicemen I had met in Canada, were taking his class and singing its praises so I started sitting in on some of those classes. It was an introduction to a Chicano history and culture I grew to love. While he was enthusiastic about the subject matter he was teaching, his underlying dissatisfaction with the way his life was going was becoming more and more apparent. We maintained contact while I moved around traveling throughout the southwest and Mexico before finding my home at the 'end of the road'. A couple of years later, Ralph followed me down to 'La Perla' after casting off academia for a simpler way of living. Reflecting on the stories presented here, I experienced nostalgia and a wide range of emotions. I thought about the people in the stories and the situations they were in. I thought about the other people on the periphery there at that time, just outside of those highlighted places. What was happening then with them and where were they now. I contacted some of the old time 'freaks' that were still living there. Who? What? Where? I was not too surprised to learn from them that very little had changed. People came and went, people died, and children were born, but there is still no store, few new houses, and the highway still ends at the lone stop sign. I wondered about the desire to leave a legacy, a wish for some part of you to remain. My thoughts went back to *The Horse in the Kitchen*, Ralph's book about his father and that way of honoring his life. Be it legacy or memoir, the story here is part of what Ralph saw, felt and left behind. Ralph Flores was a dear friend of mine. In the years we spent together in 'La Perla' and after, a bond developed that I remain thankful for and will always cherish.

Leo Bottos aka Louie
Montreal, Canada

Beely and Me

It's a cool May morning, a few minutes after sunrise, and I'm walking down a silent unpaved street at the edge of town. No one in sight, and if it weren't for the smoke rising from the stovepipes of some of the adobe houses, the town would seem deserted. Off in the distance I can hear the sheep calling excitedly to each other as Brownie, the sheep dog—the only working dog in town—herds them to the grazing fields. Avenicio's cows are lowing as he lets them out of their pens to take them to the pasture grass out toward the river, the Rio Grande, at the edge of town. Dark clouds are building to the southwest behind Ladron Peak, bringing a slight hope of rain for later in the day. Everyone in town is longing for rain to cut the heat, wash the dust out of the air, and bring new energy to the crops. But already the coolness is melting away as the sun climbs higher, and I can feel sweat running down the back of my neck and trickling down between my shoulder blades.

Another summer morning in La Perla, New Mexico.

Life in La Perla moves slowly, like someone crawling out of bed before he's fully awake, stretching languidly, smelling fresh-brewed coffee and thinking *life is good*. Listening to the bell on the bellwether ram and the lowing of the cows, and hearing hard-working Brownie barking at his charges as he herds them out of town, I feel a contentment that I'm not yet accustomed to. I still can't accept peace and harmony without feeling like they're only temporary and catastrophe and doom are waiting in ambush down the road. Life as toil, sweat, and disappointment, a blasted vale of tears. Jesus! Would I ever get away from those feelings fostered by my Catholic upbringing? Life as a vale of tears? Why would I poison my own life?

Anyway, I'm standing in the empty street, ruminating like one of Avenicio's cows, when a young couple steps out from around the corner of one of the deserted houses. He's Anglo, wearing a straight-brimmed black hat with a silver concho hatband, a pale blue shirt, and heavy brown cotton pants with a gun belt and a gun in a holster. The girl he has his left arm around is Mexican, dark eyes and darker hair, a blouse that leaves her brown arms bare, and a loose, multi-colored skirt that drapes down to her ankles, just above her bare feet. In his right arm, the man cradles a scattergun with the barrel pointed down. He raises the gun barrel when he first sees me, and then quickly lowers it again. My heart pounds. It's Billy the Kid!

"Hi Kid," I say.

He nods his head at me. "Howdy." He looks around.

"Now this is one fine, quiet little town, kinda place a fella could hide out in and nobody'd ever find him. Am I right?"

"I sure hope so, Billy. I'm looking for a place to hide too. I hope this is it, but I can't really say. I'm just visiting a friend for a couple of days."

"Say, you know where my seenyorita and me can rent a room for a few days? We gotta stop and rest for a while, get to know each other better." He pats her bottom as he talks.

She giggles and squeals: "Oh Beely!"

I shake my head. "No, not around here. This town is dying, and there's hardly anybody left. Most of the houses are abandoned and falling apart."

His eyes seem to mist over. "I guess everywhere is dying. I'm running out of places to run to. Everybody chasing me til I don't know where to go anymore. Even guys who used to be my friends are running me down. No more shelter. Nowhere."

I nod. "Yeah. If this town dies, I don't know where I'll go."

"Look," he implores, "I just want a place where I can spend what time I got left with the love of my life here"—he pats her bottom again—"while I'm still full of life and love. That aint too much to ask, is it?"

She nuzzles her face in the crook of his neck. "My Beely."

"Aint there anywhere we can go?"

"No, not anymore, least-ways not here."

He looks at me with despair. "You know, a fella has no idea where he's gonna end up once he starts the journey. He thinks he does, but he sure don't."

As I look at them they start getting blurry around the edges, like a movie a little bit out of focus. He turns to the girl. "Conchita honey, I gotta be moving.

I gotta go or they'll hunt me down." He looks at me with desperation. "*Anywhere*, anywhere at all?"

I shake my head.

Slowly, he and the girl begin to fade away.

"Billy! Don't go!" I shout. "I know there's a place for you somewhere, a haven for you and your love. And me! Take me with you. Together we can find it."

I'm standing alone in the middle of the dirt road.

Yeah. It's really *nineteen*-seventy, not eighteen-seventy, and although La Perla is real, it is a vestige from a dying past. This quiet, forgotten village is a haven for me in a world gone mad, but the winds of chaos and ignorance are blowing and dust is drifting over the landscape, over houses, cars, and people. So I felt, young and searching, in 1970.

Now, forty years later, I return to La Perla in memory.

Highway's End   Photo courtesy of Bob Christensen

La Perla

I recently saw a TV program on the "hippie movement," and the "hippie philosophy," and on the hippies' foolish idea that they could change society and transform people into loving creatures who go around singing "Kumbaya" and practicing "free love." Or something very like that. The pundits expostulating on the hippies were all relatively young, probably suckling babes in the sixties and seventies during the height of the so-called hippie movement which they were explaining to one another. One of them was an editor for the *National Review*, for Crissakes, precisely the sort of person that the so-called hippies were trying to get as far away from as they could. Listening to their babble made me start thinking about the time in my life when I was part of a back-to-the-earth migration from the cities to the countryside. I simply could not make what they were saying jibe with my own experience as a "hippie."

A few comments before we transit to La Perla. First, I never knew any dropouts to refer to themselves as "hippies." Hippie is a media word created by the media for the convenience of the media. All the people I knew called themselves "freaks," a suitable term pointing to the fact that we were social misfits, not normal, not suited to a forty-hour-a-week job or to making money. In the Middle Ages the term "freke" meant a person, a human being. If there was anything all freaks agreed on it was the idea that person-hood was what modern society was destroying. But I never heard any freak press a philosophical or political view on anyone else. I never heard a freak talk about changing or reforming society in any way, much less overthrowing the government, or any other "radical" action. All we wanted was for society to leave us alone. We believed we could set up our own "society" based on community and communal values, where people live together, cooperate, and help each other and even learn to love each other. We may seem foolish and naïve to the pundits for thinking so, but even now, more than forty years later, I don't believe we were either wrong or foolish.

La Perla (a fictional name) is literally the end of the road. About sixty-five miles south of Albuquerque, a state highway which runs north/south, parallel to the Rio Grande, atop an extended mesa which separates the low-lying, green river valley from the high desert, suddenly swoops down off the mesa and into the Rio Grande valley. As you drive off the mesa into the valley, you are struck by the dark green ribbon of the *bosque*, the forest of cottonwood, Russian olive, tamarisk, and coyote willow that borders the river. Much of what used to be farmland in La Perla has not been cultivated in years and is now bare, hard-packed dirt. There are, however, enough trees scattered throughout La Perla to provide sufficient windbreak to protect some of the topsoil, and if you supply it with seeds, fertilizer, and water, it will once again turn green and lush.

The road dips off the mesa into La Perla, runs west through town for about two hundred yards and dead-ends at a stop sign. This stop sign is the geographic center of La Perla. Past the stop sign, all the roads—to the south (left), to the north, and straight ahead—are unpaved and dusty. To the south and north, the road runs about a half-mile in each direction, beyond which there are no more houses, living or abandoned. Straight ahead about two hundred yards and running north-south, about 250 miles long and a mile wide, is the Rio Grande *bosque*, the largest cottonwood forest in the country. I have no idea why the highway department would put a stop sign at an intersection that might see four or five cars a day.

There are a few inhabited houses to the south of the sign, a few more to the north, and a few between the stop sign and the mesa to the east. There is one house and the church and its rectory to the west. There are more empty, crumbling houses than inhabited ones. Many more. The only house still standing in the center of town, at the stop sign, is a tiny two-roomer, which serves as the town post office, open from ten in the morning to eleven. Every weekday morning the post office becomes the gathering place for the entire community. The names of the people who received mail are called out, the mail distributed, and news and gossip shared. At one time there used to be a public phone booth next to the post office—then the only phone in town—but as the town faded, the phone became inoperative and the booth was overturned where it still remains lying next to the post office. There are no private businesses, no official offices, no commerce of any sort. Invariably, any strange car that drives into town is lost. Invariably, the drivers ask directions for getting to the Interstate, and invariably they are told, "You can't get there from here."

There was a time when La Perla was a thriving farming community, the largest in the area, site of the only schools—from kindergarten through high school—for miles around. Kids from Las Nutrias, Veguita, Sabinal, Concepcion, and all the other small clusters of people that comprised the rural communities surrounding La Perla went to school there. Before World War II, the Village was also the center of social life. Fiestas were always held in La Perla. It housed the only dance hall for miles around. And the only church.

The Great Depression and World War II eventually destroyed the town. Many young men left during the Depression in search of work, and never returned. And then the War started, and the young men who remained went off to fight. Those that survived came back for a short while and then left for the big city, Albuquerque, San Diego, Los Angeles. *How ya gonna keep 'em down on the farm?* The young women who did not leave with the men left on their own. Only the old timers remained, and they are dying out, crumbling like the abandoned adobe houses scattered throughout La Perla. That's the nature of an adobe house. If abandoned for a few years, the mud bricks dissolve and melt back into the earth. Eventually only a few scattered artifacts remain—a hair brush, a broken mirror, a rusted toy, a battered saucepan—melancholy ghosts of what used to be.

The effect is melancholy but also deeply satisfying: A house is built of mud bricks molded from the earth, the house is vibrant with life, the house becomes empty, and then it disappears back into the earth it arose from, and the cycle is complete. Just like with people. La Perla was becoming like the faded ruins of the Piro Indians on the East Mesa, where the desert beyond the river valley begins, right outside of town. The Piros were here before the Spaniards came. It did not take long after the arrival of the Spaniards for them to be annihilated. There is a place in the desert about a mile outside La Perla where you can see the remains of their village, the outlines of the walls where their houses used to be, and if you get down on your hands and knees you might find some of the most beautiful obsidian arrowheads you've ever seen. I suppose someday people will be sifting through the ruins of La Perla in the search for archaeological treasure, wondering what the people who lived here were like.

By the late sixties, La Perla was becoming a ghost town. There were maybe twenty people living their last days in the town. Then La Perla was "discovered" by some of the dropouts from society who were leaving the cities and fleeing into the countryside. They bought some houses for under four hundred dollars each (with electricity and indoor plumbing), and the influx of dropouts began. The town was not quite dead yet.

In 1970 I was a teaching assistant working on a PhD in American Studies at the University of New Mexico. This was a dark time for many citizens. The war in Viet Nam was a moral grinder wearing everybody down. The war split the nation in a manner unlike anything since the Civil War. You either gave whole-hearted support to the war or you were a commie pinko traitor. Nothing in-between. There were fights among conservatives and liberals, "hard hats" and "long hairs," children and parents, and students on campus. In 1970 the governor of New Mexico ordered the National Guard onto the University of New Mexico campus to break up a student antiwar protest which had closed down the school. The Guard attacked with fixed bayonets and eleven people were bayoneted, fortunately none fatally. But there were officially sanctioned killings of unarmed students on other campuses, e.g., Kent State and Jackson State.

Richard Nixon was a Mafioso disguised as President of the United States, *il capo di tuti capi*, running the country as a criminal enterprise. Before the end of his second term, Nixon's Vice President, his Chief of Staff, his Domestic Policy Advisor, the Director of the FBI, two Attorneys General, and the President's lawyer were all convicted of crimes committed while in office. And those were only the Big Fish. The majority of those convicted, the small fry, remain historically anonymous. The *Capo*-in-Chief resigned in disgrace but was pardoned by the successor president he appointed before resigning. There was, of course, moral indignation, but Nixon was too big to jail, so justice was denied the nation. Vietnam, Richard Nixon, Despair.

Violence and turmoil were ongoing. There were violent demonstrations involving racism, particularly in the late sixties with the assassination of Martin Luther King. The nation seemed on the verge of race war. Student organizations which were founded as peaceful voices for equality and reform eventually turned to violence as their only means of being heard, most significantly the Student Nonviolent Coordinating Committee and, an offshoot of Students for a Democratic Society, the Weather Underground. The nation was tearing itself apart.

Just about everybody I knew at the University was longing for escape. We fantasized about joining together and buying land as a group, leaving society and "pulling the plug," back to the earth, growing our own food, using firewood for cooking and heating, etc. None of us, of course, had any experience growing anything outside of a backyard flower garden and a couple of tomato plants, or of living without the amenities provided by modern society. It was a pipe dream, and deep down we knew it. But it was a ubiquitous dream anyway.

The word we used the most in our fantasizing was "community." We wanted to be a part of people who live together, who help and cooperate with each other, who share grief and joy and live in peace and harmony. It was this desire for community that was my driving force. I could not find community anywhere in our society. The University could become its own insular world, but it was never a satisfactory replacement for real community.

One night at a party, I met Louie, a young man who lived in a small community south of Albuquerque, a group of people who had fled the city. Here was someone who was actually doing what my friends and I only talked about! We hit it off instantly and talked for hours, while he filled my head with images of a life in La Perla that I had been dreaming of. He invited me to come visit and spend a weekend in his house in La Perla. It was time to quit talking and start doing.

I visited Louie in La Perla the next weekend and fell in love with the town. I entered a time I thought had died with the onslaught of the Twentieth Century and the Industrial Revolution. No cars on the road, no telephones, no televisions, no radios blaring bubblegum rock, no convenience stores: A fulfillment of the monastery fantasies which always lay just beneath my surface. When I told Louie I was thinking of quitting my job and moving to La Perla, he offered to let me stay in his house until I could find a place of my own.

"I want a divorce," she said. "I knew he was going to twist your life around."

And so it happened. My wife left and started divorce proceedings. I informed the University that this was my last semester, and at semester's end, I went to La Perla and moved in with Louie, where a section of his living room became my space until I could find my own house. Unfortunately, my money had gone with my divorce, and I didn't have enough to buy a three hundred and fifty dollar home should I find one for sale. But Louie was generous and glad to have someone living with him. My excitement was palpable. The University and the city and their frustrations were dissolving from my memory.

We who fled to La Perla really thought we could find or create a sane, harmonious place to live and work alongside others, and turn back the clock to a simpler, more innocent time. Okay, so there never was a "simpler" time of innocence, but the idea was seductive nonetheless. *Innocence!* Now, years later, I understand that innocence was a key word for me. When you lose your innocence, is it irretrievably lost? I know I can never be a child again with a child's innocence, but is there some form of innocence that can be retained as we age? For me, *innocence* took the form of believing in people again, in their essential goodness, in their desire to live a good life, to shoulder common responsibilities for the community, to help and support each other, and yes, to love each other too. We thought you could do your own thing as long as you did not infringe upon others. It was that simple. Whether our attempt was successful or a failure depends on how one defines "success."

What I remember most about my life in La Perla were the

many different people I met there. Some were old-timers whose families had lived there for generations, some were visitors, some resident freaks—like me, young and dissatisfied with the lives they had been living. As different as the freaks were from each other, they all shared that dissatisfaction. Everybody was searching for something that contemporary society did not, for whatever reasons, provide for them. But living harmoniously with others in your daily life can be very difficult. It sounds simple enough, but to accomplish harmony with others requires getting rid of so much of one's pettiness, and that which is petty—ego, ingrained bad habits, selfishness, distrust, cynicism—is often the most difficult of all things to eradicate. La Perla was a filter which separated those who truly wanted community from those who thought they wanted it, but for their own reasons were incapable of grasping it.

Post Office   Photo courtesy of Bob Christensen

La Perla People

When I first came to La Perla there was a hard core of freaks, most of whom had been living there for about one year. Joel and Tommy were the first freaks to come live in La Perla. Joel had a Masters in math and a PhD in psychology. Tommy was a recovering heroin addict. They had driven across country together, from Lexington, Kentucky, where Joel had been a drug therapist and counselor in the federal rehab center in Lexington, and Tommy had been one of his patients, rehabbing from a heroin addiction. Tommy turned Joel on to marijuana and then supplied him with weed thereafter. They eventually took LSD together, and under its influence, Joel decided to quit his job and take to the road, and Tommy went with him. The two of them, and Shep, Tommy's German Shepard, headed west in Joel's old, beat up Mercedes, until they got lost in New Mexico, and wound up at the stop sign in the middle of La Perla. It was the end of the road, so they stayed. They contacted the absentee owners of a couple of derelict adobe houses and were told that if they resurrected the houses, they could live in them rent free. They set to work immediately. Shortly after I arrived, Sara, a slender, doe-eyed, serene lady moved in with Joel. And Tommy also established a somewhat uneasy relationship with a young woman who moved in with him, as I detail later in this narrative.

The next to get lost and drive into La Perla were Ron and Cindy. She was from the upper-scale Cleveland suburb of Shaker

Heights, and he was from a semi-disreputable neighborhood in the city. As teenagers, they met at a rock concert and became lovers. He was just what she wanted in her rebellion against upper-middle class life in Shaker Heights. He was everything her parents feared for their daughter—a high-school dropout with no job and no "future." But he was a pretty good mechanic and had a VW Beetle, and they drove west into the sunset. For him, I suppose she represented what had always seemed unattainable, the girl at the other end of the socio-economic scale. He was bright, and like many self-educated people, he knew a little about a lot of things, and often made a point of demonstrating his knowledge. She was redheaded, voluptuous, and docile, almost bovine. But she did have enough spirit to rebel against her parents, although now she let Ron make most of their decisions.

Louie was Canadian but had been living in the U.S. illegally for five years. At eighteen, he had set out from Canada with his inheritance money from his father's death, and traveled all around the Mediterranean world, living in international "hippie" colonies on various Aegean islands. He returned to the U.S. and traveled aimlessly until he met Joel at a party in Albuquerque and found out about La Perla. He moved in and bought a two-bedroom house with electricity and indoor plumbing on three quarters of an acre. A few months after I moved in with him, Karen, a friend of a friend of Louie's from San Francisco, came to visit La Perla. She was a legal secretary in San Francisco on vacation, and like so many other young visitors to La Perla, she became enchanted with the town. She stayed and moved in with Louie.

Jill was a petite lady with an iron will. She too had been a teaching assistant at the University of New Mexico, where we had met and, in those weeks before my last semester was over, became occasional lovers. A couple months after I quit my job and left the city, she too quit and moved to La Perla. Of all the dropouts in the community, she was the most dropped. She kept disengaging herself from all the "conveniences" of modern society, and even though she had a house in La Perla, she eventually put up a teepee and moved into it. When the freaks who lived in the mountains some thirty miles away moved into the valley to spend the winter, she would take down her teepee and move into the mountains and live in the snow, alone, until the weather warmed up and the mountain freaks came back. She would then return to La Perla. As small as she was, she was a farrier, and once traveled along the mountain peaks of the Continental Divide from Colorado into Mexico with only a burro as a companion.

Len and Amy were the ambiguous members. They came shortly after Louie. They had been married for three years. He was working construction and she was studying to be a teacher when they dropped out. He wanted to farm, so they bought a farmhouse and twenty acres on the outskirts of La Perla. I don't think they saw themselves as freaks the same way the rest of us saw ourselves. Like the rest of us, they were discontented with modern society, but their move to La Perla was a change of occupation and lifestyle, from construction to farming. They came to the communal dinners and feasts but remained on the outer fringes of the group where we'd find them when we needed to borrow an egg or a cup of milk.

There was a continual stream of misfits and discontents who would come, move into an empty house, stay for two or three months, sometimes longer, and then leave. Mostly I think they found life in La Perla too difficult and too different from what they were used to. When you heat and cook with firewood, it takes a lot of time and work to keep a constant supply of fuel on hand. One of the symbols of security in La Perla was not having a lot of cash but rather having a large stack of cut firewood next to your house. Growing your own food was another time-consuming enterprise. You had to have manure and compost, you had to water and weed your garden, you had to keep out the hungry varmints and insects which saw your garden as their little Eden. And, of course, there were difficulties in maintaining smooth relationships with others. These temporary residents were a cross-section of the disaffected and discontented of our society. There was nothing *wrong* with them; they just didn't fit into modern society, but for whatever reasons were incapable of changing their situation.

La Perla was a sort of ink blot test for visitors. People saw what they wanted or expected to see when they first visited. The young saw a group of people living in a harmonious and cooperative community, something missing from their lives, something they yearned for. They would walk around saying, "Boy, I wish I could live here. It's so peaceful!"

Our reaction to these comments was two-fold. First, it was *not* peaceful in La Perla. Underneath the peaceful patina were emotional turmoil, flashes of anger, disputes, personal relationships in constant turmoil, and never-ending accommodations to the needs and wants of others. Our society does not prepare us for cooperation and compromise. Everything is a zero-sum game: If I win, you have to lose, and *vice versa*. Why can't we all be winners?

Second, we felt that if you really wanted to drop out and move to La Perla, you would do so. Ultimately, you do what you really want to do. Everything else is just talk. We never tried talking anyone into joining us. The only thing holding people back was fear—fear of having no steady income, or a greatly reduced income; fear of finding out who you are when you don't have a job by which you can identify *what* you are and verify your worth to society; fear of giving up some of your rights and freedom for the sake of harmony and community; fear of intimacy with the Other; and a general fear of letting the future come to you in whatever form it takes.

So whenever anyone said they wished they could live in La Perla, our response was a silent shrug.

Then why did I, and the others, eventually leave this haven? What drove us away and apart? One thing the freaks all had in common when I moved to La Perla was the absolute conviction that we would never, *could* never, return to mainstream society, and we could never change it; we just wanted it to leave us alone. We had a little island we lived in and were happy there. I've thought about why it fell apart and why we left to re-enter a world we had tried so hard to run away from. Ultimately, I think we all learned that it is possible to live in modern society without feeling trapped. As the Sufis say, "Be *in* the world, but not *of* the world."

TV in La Perla

Although my plan was to cut loose from all my "material possessions," as I referred to my car, my color TV, expensive sound equipment, and books, the terms of my divorce were such that I wound up with all of those things since my ex-wife, now in Florida, did not want to bother with having them sent to her or to come pick them up herself. So I arrived in La Perla with these possessions. I not only had the only television set in La Perla, it was a *color* TV, not that common in 1970. I just assumed that I would store these things in someone's shed until I could sell them for a few bucks.

To my surprise and disgust, the TV created quite a stir among the freaks in town. It was immediately hooked up in Louie's house, and the freaks came in daily to watch the soap operas. I said nothing for a few days—it was, after all, Louie's house, not mine—but finally I complained about the TV going almost constantly.

"What are you bitching about?" asked Tommy, a slender man with long black hair and piercing eyes. "*You* brought the television with you. Why'd you bring it if you didn't want it hooked up?"

"I didn't want it. It was part of my divorce settlement, and I brought it with me until I could sell it and the other stuff."

"You think somebody in La Perla's going to buy it?"

"Of course not, but I just wanted to settle in before I tried to sell it, maybe in Belen or Albuquerque."

"If I don't want something, I get rid of it. I don't carry it around with me until I find the right place to dump it. I don't want it, I don't keep it."

"OK, OK, so maybe I should have thrown it away and didn't. But it's still my TV and I don't want it going all the time."

"Why should you care what I do with my time? If I want to watch TV, why should that piss you off? If you don't want to watch TV, don't. What's simpler than that? Why lay your trip on me?"

The situation was very confusing. What I wanted to say was, "I thought we were all trying to get away from television and all the other bullshit of modern society," but maybe I was wrong. The other freaks may have had completely different reasons for living here. Maybe some were just here because they fell into this sort of life and didn't really know what they wanted. But then maybe I didn't know what I wanted, maybe Tommy was right—if I had really wanted to get rid of the TV, I would have done so before I came to La Perla.

There was a "free store" set up in a shed in La Perla. The freaks from all the surrounding area brought in extra clothes, appliances, tools, and left them and took whatever they needed in exchange. No one tended the store and no money was ever exchanged. You left what was superfluous and took what you needed. I wonder now why I didn't take my TV there and let it end up in someone else's house in La Perla so I wouldn't have to listen to it. Now, though, I just tune it out.

The TV ended up in Louie's bathtub.

Sex and the Single Male

For single men, living in La Perla was somewhat like living in a monastery. There was a shortage of unattached women, which resulted in an involuntary abstinence. Single men in La Perla often led chaste lives, but not from choice. Unlike a straight person's fantasies about "hippie sexual freedom," couples in the group were generally monogamous. "Bird dogging" another man's lady was not acceptable. Oh, there might be an occasional "indiscretion," a single man and a woman who was half a couple might find themselves alone and in a spirit of spontaneous warmth and affection, they make love. But that was not common. Unrestricted sex could be dynamite, blowing up friendships, love relationships, and general civility.

The isolation of La Perla was what attracted many of us to the community, but it was also the cause of unease. It was fifteen lonely miles to the nearest convenience store, and twenty-five miles to the nearest real town. Considering that most of the people in La Perla had no functioning vehicles, the isolation was quite real.

"Too much *yang* energy, and not enough *yin*," the freaks would say, a male and female imbalance which could produce tension among the males, especially when an unattached female came to visit. The competition to impress her could be pretty intense.

"Men without women are like a bunch of rocks," Joel, who had a PhD in psychology, would say. "They're hard and rough-edged. Women are the rock tumblers, and eventually they round out the sharp edges of the men. If you're lucky."

This is the environment that Lily stepped into about two weeks after I had moved in with Louie.

Lily was from Albuquerque, a friend of Louie's who had recently broken up with her live-in companion. After a few weeks of feeling blue and moping around, she decided to get away from the city and come visit Louie, a good friend, for a few days. She was intelligent, vivacious, with dark hair and eyes and a wonderful sense of humor. She was also Voluptuous with a capital "V." A truly lovely woman.

Word spread quickly that a single woman, a lovely woman, was visiting Louie, and soon every single male freak was dropping in, gentlemen callers come to make the acquaintance of the new lady. In addition to Louie and me were Tommy, Joel, Larry, and Frank. At first Lily seemed overwhelmed by all the attention, but she soon began to enjoy it and play off it with the hint of a smile. She was now in control. Tommy invited her to his house for dinner that evening, but in order to keep the peace, he had to invite all the other single men too.

Lily planned to stay a few days, so Louie had given up his bed and room for her and was sleeping in a bedroll next to mine on the living-room floor. That evening, to get ready for the dinner party, Lily went into her room and a half hour later came out dressed in a form-fitting, floor length, green velvet dress with gold trim and a scooped-out front that revealed deep cleavage. Both Louie and I tried to act normal, but we could not take our eyes off her as she walked around in the house.

The three of us walked to Tommy's, at the southern end of town, at sunset. Tommy had made eggplant parmigiano and corn bread. Joel had brought a garden salad. The food was good and the conversation at dinner was animated and loud, with much laughter, pot smoking and wine-drinking.

During a break in the talk, Tommy leaned back in his chair, looked directly at Lily and asked "Have you noticed that there are six men here and only one woman?"

Lily laughed. "Yeah, that sort of caught my attention."

"That's 'cause all the women who live in La Perla are already living with guys. It's hard to find a woman who's willing to live here permanently. Women come and think it looks like a great place to live, and they might stay a few days, maybe even a month, or even two, but they always go back to the city. So when a pretty woman comes to visit, all the guys get excited and try to hang out around her."

"Wait a minute," said Louie. "I didn't come to dinner because I want to convince Lily to stay in La Perla. She's a good friend and a good person, and I like being around her." He looked at Lily and smiled. She smiled back.

"I'm here because of the good food," said Joel. "If I eat here, then I don't have cook my own dinner."

Tommy snorted. "Yeah, right. All you're interested in is the food."

"And why is it that most women don't want to stay permanently?" asked Lily.

Tommy shrugged. "We're isolated here. The nearest town is twenty-five miles away, and it aint much of a town. Albuquerque is sixty-five miles. Women don't like being so far away from 'civilization.' After a few days here, they realize how hard it is to live without gas stoves, cars, central heating, television, and all those other things the city offers. Once they realize how hard it is to gather firewood, for example, and cut it, split it, store it, and then cook and heat with it, they pack it up and leave. And that's just firewood."

"Wait a minute," said Lily with an arched eyebrow. "Are you saying that men can handle this "rugged life" and women can't?"

"Men and women are basically different," responded Tommy. "Women have babies, so they want a nice 'nest' just in case they get pregnant, and they want to be near doctors and hospitals.

The nearest doctor here is in Socorro, about twenty-five miles away. That's too far for women."

"What a bunch of bullshit! Women have lived far from cities and had babies for centuries and centuries. Women have planted and harvested crops, preserved food, hauled water, cooked your meals, stroked your fucking frail egos, done all the things men in the country do in *addition to* having babies. What you're saying is just male chauvinist crap." She was glaring at Tommy.

"I'm just telling you what I see here in La Perla. *You* tell me why women won't stay here when they say they like it so much," Tommy prodded.

"I've only been here one day, but I think I have a pretty good idea why. After talking with you, I think they just don't like the men who are here. Maybe they don't like their attitude. Maybe the men here are trying hard to be macho, pretending they're hot shit because they live in the country and cut firewood. I come here to visit an old friend, and every single guy in town comes over trying to be 'sexy.' Sure that can be fun, but it also makes me feel like a prize cow at auction. I'll tell you what impresses me: Guys who don't try to impress me. Show me something real, not this trying to impress me crap."

Tommy grinned. "Why should I even want to impress you? You say the guys here think they're hot shit, but what about you thinking I'm hot to impress you?"

I was really surprised at Tommy's aggression toward Lily. She sat across from him, her jaw clenched, her lips a thin, red line as she glared into his eyes. "The last thing on my mind is trying to impress you. And don't tell me that when you came to Louie's this afternoon you were not trying to be a cock rooster strutting in front of a hen. You're as good a reason for a woman not wanting to stay here as I can imagine."

The rest of us had been sitting quietly, watching Tommy and Lily spar with each other. There was a tense moment of silence, and then Tommy grinned, picked up the wine bottle and asked Lily if she wanted a refill. Still glaring at him, she held out her glass.

After that, the dinner went by quietly, but I could still feel the crackling tension between Lily and Tommy. No matter who was talking or what was being talked about, I could see that the two of them were mostly conscious of each other in a hard, unblinking way.

We walked slowly back to Louie's afterwards, nobody talking. Soon after we got home, Lily went to bed while Louieand I stayed up for a while. Louie paced up and down in the living room, muttering as he made his circuit, "She's so beautiful, she's so beautiful." He glanced at me sheepishly. "What a pretty lady," he said. I shrugged and went to bed.

The next morning Joel was driving into Albuquerque, and Lily decided to cut her visit short and return to the city with him.

"After last night with Tommy," sighed Louie, "I can't say that I blame her. It was like he was trying to chase her off." He shook his head.

As they were getting ready to leave, Tommy showed up and asked for a ride into town. He said he just wanted to get away for a few days in the "fleshpots of the city," as he put it. They got into the car and drove up onto the mesa in Joel's beat up Volvo, away from La Perla.

"Well," said Louie, "There goes another one. Tommy scared her off."

"Maybe we all did," I said, "acting like a bunch of flies buzzing around a bowl of sugar."

Three days later, the Volvo came back down the mesa into town carrying Joel, Tommy, and Lily. Joel drove directly to Tommy's house, where Tommy carried a suitcase with Lily's clothes inside, with Lily following.

"I don't get it," said Louie, shaking his head. "I just don't get it. Does she want to have a power struggle with him, show him how tough she can be, or is she really attracted to him? I guess Tommy's right. Men and women are just too different to really understand each other. Such a pretty lady!"

Homecoming

Two months in La Perla, two months of living without a regular job, without newspapers, radio or TV news, cut off totally from my previous life of schedules and time-bound responsibilities. I had gone from the circumscribed world of the university where all events were abstractions—literature, history, science, society, people—were all concepts, ideas to be mulled over and debated—to the even smaller world of La Perla where the conceptual was virtually nonexistent. Everything was concrete. Nobody talked about ideals, about visions of how life should be lived; instead we concerned ourselves with getting the money to buy the saw to build the additional shelves for the kitchen, and the nails and screws and wood. . . .

Without my being consciously aware of it, the war in Vietnam had receded to the backstairs of my mind. And grotesque as he was, Nixon was not to be taken seriously. He was just another power-hungry clown in a long line of clowns whose time would come and pass. Without the daily fix of news, the news of the day no longer played a role in my daily life. Ironically, in the laid back world of La Perla, there was no time to concern ourselves with events beyond our small boundaries. No one ever talked about Nixon or cursed the war in Viet Nam. We talked about keeping mice and rabbits out of our gardens, dealing with squash bugs and other pests, getting enough water for our gardens from the overloaded, Rube Goldberg water system the community used and which regularly broke down. We dealt with problems we could actually do something about, problems we could fix and feel good about fixing. We stayed focused on our community and let the rest of the world go. You want to fuck up your world? That's your business. Just include me out. "Be here now," Tommy used to say, "and be there later." A very selfish view, but for the first time in years I was not depressed. I felt that I was living like a human being and not like the consumer society wanted me to be.

After two months I had a plan and was working to make said plan reality. I started with a post and rail fence to mark off my space from the rest of Louie's property and to make a place for the garden I would plant next spring.

I was sweating in the summer heat digging the holes for the fence posts when I saw a blue Volkswagen bus come down off the east mesa into town. It stopped in front of Louie's. I dropped the post-hole digger and went around to see who it was. Going around the corner of Louie's house I bumped into Jill.

She hugged me, and then exulted. "I did it! I did it! I quit my teaching assistant job at the University and I'm moving here! Everything I own is in my bus."

"You're moving here? Why?"

"I want to change my life too. I realized I couldn't keep on doing what I was doing. I was spending my whole life getting a degree I don't really want to do something I don't want to do." She hugged me again. "So, here I am!"

"You certainly are. I'm surprised."

"Yeah, it's still a surprise to me. I didn't know I was coming until yesterday, when I started packing my stuff."

"How long will you be visiting?"

"Oh, I'm not visiting. I'm moving here! Everything I own is in my bus."

"You're moving here? Wow! This is really unexpected. I just don't know what to say."

Louie came out and hugged Jill. Still bubbling with excitement, she told Louie what her plans were. He reacted with joy. "That's great! But we have to find a place for you to stay."

Lily and Tommy had left on a hitchhiking trip the day before. As often happened with the freaks, they left without any idea where they were going or when they were coming back. They just had the urge to go. Their house was currently empty, and like all the freaks, they had no lock on the doors. So, on the assumption that they would not begrudge a fellow freak a place to stay, Jill was moved into their house until she could find her own place.

I was shocked by her arrival. I was no longer devastated by my divorce, and I was enjoying being free and unattached. But now, what expectations did she have about a relationship? Louie was the only person from La Perla that Jill knew, so I felt obligated to take her around and introduce her to the other freaks. I felt uneasy since my being with her would suggest that we were a couple. A welcoming dinner was planned at Louie's house, and sure enough, by the end of the evening the pressure pushing us together was more than I could resist. I spent the night with Jill in Tommy and Lily's bed.

I was lying in Tommy and Lily's bed. It was a hot midsummer morning and the sheets were damp with perspiration. I could hear Jill moving about in the kitchen, slamming drawers and rattling dishes and pans. She came into the room, yanked open a dresser drawer, rustled around in it, and then slammed it shut. I lay in bed trying to recall what it was I said or did last night that precipitated this response. I could tell this was a bad one, and the rage would probably last for days. I lay totally depressed.

I forced myself to get up. I was not eager to face another day with this woman. I dressed slowly, deliberately, and then walked out the front door. She was sitting on the step crying soundlessly and looked away toward the east mesa and the desert beyond when I stepped gingerly around her and out into the bright sunlight. We made no attempt to speak to each other.

I went to my car and sat in it for a few minutes, gripping the steering wheel tightly until the constriction in my throat broke loose and I hit the steering wheel hard with my open hand. I got out of the car and walked over to her. She was still on the step, no longer crying, mouth pursed and tight.

"I'm leaving," I said. "Now, this morning."

She looked at me, poker faced, blank.

"I'm not coming back," I warned.

She turned away, again looking at the mesa. "I don't have any money," she said, "and I don't have anywhere else to go."

I went into the house, grabbed my wallet off the dresser, and went outside and gave her fifty dollars, noting the dwindling remnants of my last paycheck from the University.

She took the money without comment, balled it up in her fist, and turned back to the desert in the east. I hurried into the house, dumped some clothes in a cardboard box, and walked past her to my car. Now that I had started, I was anxious to get on the road. I drove away without looking back.

After that everything became a blur. I drove west, going all day until I got sleepy late that night, and then I pulled off onto the roadside and slept in the cramped backseat of my VW Beetle. I rose at daybreak and continued driving west until I hit the California coast. I then drove north along the coast, picking up hitchhikers and taking them wherever they wanted to go, continuing generally north until I got to Portland, Oregon. I stayed a week in Portland, living with two freaks I met on the road and then headed back along Highway One to San Francisco. There, two things happened: My car got sick and started coughing and sputtering, and my money ran out.

I parked my ailing car in the Haight-Ashbury District and walked to Golden Gate Park. I walked around the park for a couple of hours, unable to come up with a plan for my next move. I had no experience with being homeless and felt scared. I was in a funk of complete helplessness.

Sitting on a bench in the park, I looked across the street. On the wall facing me someone had written:
ONLY ACTION OVERCOMES FEAR.

I stared at the sign for a moment before the message penetrated. *Don't just sit here; do something. What am I scared of? I'm not going to die; I just have to take control. I have as much right to a place on this earth as a deer or a hawk or a rabbit. Do something! Move!*

I went back to my car, managed to get it started, and drove toward the ocean. I was limping along the coast again when I saw a sign for the San Francisco Zoo. On impulse I drove into the parking lot. I checked my pockets and found I still had enough money to buy a ticket. I paid and entered.

I wandered around, looking morosely at the caged animals, telling myself I had a kinship with them. They saddened me, and feeling depressed again, I slumped down on a bench. In a moment I noticed that on the other end of the bench was a slender young woman eating a sack lunch. She was blond and attractive, and the sight of her sitting there eating was almost painful to me. She looked over at me and, to my astonishment, smiled. Automatically, I smiled back.

"Have you seen the wolves?" she asked.

"What? Uh, no. I've just been wandering around for a few minutes. I guess I haven't seen much of the zoo."

"Come on. I'll show you the wolves." She stood up and waited for me to follow her.

I went with her, stunned at her initiating the contact. *God, I must be a sight, and she's so clean and pretty.* She led me to the gate that said EMPLOYEES ONLY and opened it.

"I work here. I'm on my lunch break. My name's Carol." She held out her hand.

I shook it. "Raf," I responded.

We went through the gate, and she led me to two large holding pens enclosed by a chain-link fence. In one of the pens was a cheetah and in the other, two grey wolves.

"The exhibits for these animals aren't ready yet," she said. "I come here every day. I love the wolves. That is Romeo and this is Juliet."

She reached into her paper bag, pulled something out, and knelt down. She held it in her finger tips and stuck it through the fence. Juliet came over and took it in her mouth and ate it. Carol stretched her fingers and stroked the wolf's fur. Romeo walked over to the fence that separated them from the cheetah. The cheetah trotted over beside him and the two animals began running back and forth together with the fence between them. They had worn a path on either side. I watched Carol stroking Juliet while Romeo and the cheetah ran frantically.

Carol stood up. "They're so beautiful. They're my special friends." She turned to face me. "What are you doing here?"

"I ran away from home," I said, laughing and feeling foolish. "I'm from New Mexico. I guess I don't know what I'm doing here."

"Are you married?"

"No."

She looked at me closely. "Do you know anybody in San Francisco? Do you have any money? Do you have a place to stay?"

"No."

She started heading back to the gate. "I have to go back to work. I'm a secretary in the front office. I really want to work with the animals, though."

Not knowing what else to do, I followed along. She led me to a large building, and then stopped and turned. "I get off work at five."

"Ok."

I spent the afternoon at the beach, a short walk from the zoo.

At five I went back to the zoo and waited in the parking lot outside the main entrance. After about fifteen minutes she came out and smiled when she saw me.

"I was expecting you to be outside the main office. When I didn't see you, I thought maybe you had left."

Embarrassed, I told her I had lost my ticket stub and didn't have enough money to buy another. She shook her head and laughed. Once again, I got my car running and followed her to her apartment. Inside, I showered, then helped her cook dinner.

We made some small talk. At first there were periods of awkward silence, but as we worked together the talk got easier.

Soon I was telling her about teaching at the University and about life in La Perla, without mentioning Jill. She told me she had been divorced for eight months following a five-year marriage. The divorce had been hard on her, and she had shied away from men afterward.

"Yeah, I know," she said. "I'm the one who started the conversation with you at the zoo." She laughed. "You looked so much like a lost puppy that I couldn't resist."

"A lost puppy!" I played indignant.

"Ok. How about a caged wolf?" We both laughed.

After eating, she went into the bathroom, then stuck her head out the door.

"I don't do this kind of thing as a matter of habit." And then by way of explanation, "You really remind me of someone I knew in high school."

I sat thumbing through some old *Time* magazines until she stepped out in a cloud of stem, wrapped in a towel. I stood and we faced each other awkwardly. I moved to her and we embraced. She led me to her bedroom and we went to bed.

For the next few days I walked around San Francisco while she was at work. In the evenings we talked about our respective days, made dinner and then went to bed. She had been absent from men long enough that she was always eager for me.

That weekend we went driving north of the city and stopped for a stroll through a large grove of trees. The trees were bay laurels, and as we walked on the fallen leaves the aroma of the bay leaves rose up and enveloped us. We stopped on a shady slope and made love, crushing the leaves beneath our twisting bodies.

For me it seemed perfect. Here was a beautiful, warm, intelligent woman who had removed any concerns I might have had about food and shelter, and whose only demands on me were sexual. And I really liked her. For some reason, I was sure it couldn't last—maybe it was just too good—but for now it was perfect.

On the Monday following our first weekend together, I was heading back to her apartment from one of my walks around the city when I heard a voice cursing loudly from beneath an old school bus parked on the street with the hood up. A head poked out from underneath the front end of the bus and looked up at me.

"Can I talk you into giving me a hand for a moment?" he asked.

I stopped and knelt down. "Sure."

"I'm trying to line up some holes so I can bolt the water pump to the block, but I gotta have three hands to do it. There's a big screwdriver on the fender. Can you use it to pry up the pump and I'll let you know when the holes are lined up?"

In a few minutes we were done, and a young man crawled out from under the bus. He wiped his hand on his pants and held it out. "Thanks. I'm Jamie."

"I'm Raf."

Jamie looked at me for a moment. "Do you want to smoke a joint?" he asked, gesturing with his head toward the Victorian house the bus was parked in front of.

Jamie took me in the house and we got stoned. "I'm a trader," he said. "I deal in American Indian jewelry, Navajo rugs, and ironwood carvings from the Seri Indians down in Mexico. Been doing it for about two years. The bus is my traveling headquarters. You live in San Francisco?"

Stoned, I found it easy to talk about my divorce, quitting my job, living in La Perla, Jill, and my current situation with Carol.

Jamie was from Phoenix and was staying with a friend in this house while he got the bus in good running condition. He told me that his own marriage was rocky, and he and his wife had been living apart for about a week.

"I found out she had been sleeping with a friend of mine for about a year. I felt betrayed, but she kept telling me a lot of it was my own fault for the way I treated her. Said she was tired of being treated like a servant, or like a spoiled kid treats his mother, always expecting her to do everything for me. We went round and round. Anyway, we decided to stay away from each other for about a month, and then see if we want to try to patch it."

"It's going to be hard to do," I responded. "Divorce is a lot easier."

Jamie pulled out a cigarette and stuck it in a long ivory cigarette holder. "But the thing for me is, I really don't want to leave Sharon, and I don't think she wants to leave me. Or so she tells me. Hell, if she had come up and told me she wanted to fuck Mike, I probably would have gone along with it. But it's weird when things aren't the way you thought they were for a year or so. You start remembering all the times the three of you were together, and you start seeing secret meanings in what they said or in their gestures, and suddenly you're pissed off again."

"So why do you want to stay with her?"

He lit the cigarette with a lighter inlaid with turquoise and red coral and took a deep drag. "I love her, man. And she's right about the way I've been treating her. I thought a lot about that. See, I had the perfect mom when I was a kid. My mom did everything I wanted. She lived her life for her kids. I guess I grew up thinking that's what women were supposed to be like."

"But can you trust her? I mean, will you be able to?"

Jamie took another drag and exhaled a long stream of smoke up toward the ceiling. "There's the rub, right? Sharon is a beautiful woman. Lots of guys would like to go with her. But what the hell, I like having beauty around me. That's why I have trouble getting ahead as a trader—I keep the best stuff for myself. Why would anyone want to have ugly or mediocre things around? Look at this room, at that print on the wall, or that couch—they're ugly, really ugly. It makes me uncomfortable to be around ugly things." He gestured so violently at the print on the wall the cigarette came flying out of the holder. "But if I want a beautiful wife, then I guess other guys are going to want her too. My ego and my desire for beauty are going to have to fight this one out."

He paused to reload the cigarette holder. His hands were shaking so badly he was struggling to get the cigarette in. He noticed me watching his hands. He broke into a violent hacking cough.

"I had polio when I was a kid," explained Jamie. "Thought I was going to die. I got over it, except my hands shake and my legs are a little weak. It was when I was lying in bed with the polio that I realized how much I hated ugly things."

"Where is your wife now?"

"She stayed in Phoenix and when my pickup died, I went up to Seattle to buy this bus from a lesbian couple I met in Arizona. For five hundred bucks I got a complete home on wheels. I'm starting on a trip across Nevada and Arizona. I'll be doing some buying and selling, but mostly I just want to be traveling for a while. Should take about a month. Then I'll head back to Phoenix and talk with Sharon."

"Well, I wish you luck," I said. "I think you'll need it."

Jamie looked at me intently, then pointed the cigarette holder at me with a flourish. "Hey, I like your vibe. You want to go traveling? I'm looking for someone to go on my next trip with me just for companionship. You interested?"

"I don't have any money."

Jamie laughed. "Hey, I don't either! Not much, anyway. But I've got my basic stock of jewelry and rugs. I just sell them or trade on the road and use the money to buy food and gas and more jewelry and rugs. Unless I find something really special. That kinda stuff I keep."

I said I would think about it and gave Jamie Carol's phone number. We agreed to talk the next day.

That night, after we made love, I told Carol about meeting Jamie and Jamie's offer. She lay in the dark, listening quietly.

"You know," she said, "you don't owe me anything. I mean you're free to do whatever you want. If you want to go with Jamie, that's OK." She paused for a moment. "If you want to stay here, that's OK too." She lifted up, leaning on her elbows. "I talked to Mac today. He's my boss. He thinks there's a good chance he can get you on at the zoo, feeding animals and cleaning cages and stuff like that. It wouldn't pay much, but you could stay here, and we could split expenses."

I said I would think about that. So I lay in bed weighing my options. I enjoyed Carol's company, she was beautiful, and so far we had gotten along well. And the love-making was passionate. But was I ready for another relationship with a woman? My experience with my wife and with Jill had left me feeling snake-bit. If I stayed, there would soon be obligations, responsibilities, expectations. Jamie was offering me freedom. No cares. Just travel around in a crazy school bus with a green Hindu elephant painted on one side, and Mr. Zigzag from the Zigzag cigarette rolling papers printed on the back door. Maybe this was the chance to find myself, the new beginning I had been looking for since I quit teaching at the University. I was mulling these thoughts when I fell asleep.

The next morning I had still not made up my mind when Carol left for work. Around ten o'clock that morning Jamie called me.

"Hey, what you wanna do? You wanna come with?"

My answer blurted out. "Yeah. I wanna go with you."

"Great! We'll leave tomorrow morning."

We made arrangements to meet the next day, and then I spent the rest of the day watching TV and fretting about telling Carol when she came home later.

When she got home she did not ask me about my decision. I knew she was anxious to know, and her discretion made me momentarily wonder if I was making the wrong choice in deciding to leave her. I told her during dinner, and she took it very well, made it clear there were no bad feelings and no holds on me.

"Will you keep in touch?" she asked.

"Of course!"

"How can I contact you if I want to?"

"I'm not sure where I'll be. I guess the closest thing to an address that I have is care of Louie Caputti, General Delivery, La Perla, New Mexico."

That night, for the first time since we had been together, we did not make love. We both said we were just too tired. The next morning Carol left for work with a kiss and my promise to write to her. I then went through my car, cleaning everything out of it until there was nothing that could connect the car to me. I got it started and drove it to the Rapid Transit parking lot a few blocks away. I parked it and walked back to Carol's, got my backpack, and went to Jamie's. Before noon, we were on our way to Nevada.

For the next four weeks we traveled the highways and back roads of Nevada and Arizona, sometimes pulling off the road at night to sleep, other times staying in campgrounds. Since it was now after Labor Day, the campgrounds were never crowded. Whenever we needed money, we would go around to the various campsites carrying jewelry from the Navajos, the New Mexico Pueblos, the Hopis, and the Zunis. For the first time in my life, I felt free of worry and obligations. There was no schedule. If we liked a place, we would stay there extra days before moving on. Whenever we saw a place that looked interesting, we would stop, even if we had only traveled ten or fifteen miles from our previous stop.

As we traveled, we often picked up hitchhikers and talked to all sorts of people. *My god*, I thought, *America is on the move. All these people unhappy with the lives they've been living, on the road looking for something.* We picked up an itinerant preacher, underage runaways, the homeless with no destination, hippies going to one commune or another—legions of people on the move. One couple we picked up was in their late thirties. She had been an elementary school teacher and he a high school teacher in Falls Church, Virginia. One day they confessed their unhappiness with their whole existence to each other, and since they had no children, they quit their jobs, bought a motorcycle, and set off west to look for purpose and meaning. Their bike required some repairs and they were on their way to town to buy parts.

There was no way to categorize the people on the road, no particular age group, financial status, or educational level. The only common denominator seemed to be the search for something other than what they had. And I could never tell what kind of person someone would turn out to be from appearance. Once in Zion National Park we struck up a conversation with a couple camped next to us in a top-of-the-line RV. They seemed excruciatingly straight, he in brand new Levis and flannel shirt and she in a beehive hairdo and slacks. We invited them over for coffee, and they accepted. Once we had the coffee brewed, Jamie began his pitch to sell some jewelry. While examining a bracelet, the man, Donnie, suddenly asked if we had any "*paiote*."

For a moment we were at a loss. Then Jamie understood: "Peyote! He exclaimed. "You want some peyote?"

"Well," said Donnie, "Me and Charlene have read a lot about it—y'all ever read Carlos Castaneda?— but we've never tried it." He looked a little embarrassed. "We'd like to try it, but we don't know how to get any."

Jamie and I looked at each other, wondering if these were narcs. "We don't have any peyote, and I sure don't know where you can get some."

"We have some pot," said Charlene. "Y'all want to get stoned?"

We all went over to the RV and got stoned. Donnie and Charlene lived in an expensive area of San Luis Obispo and had started smoking dope as "an experiment." They liked it and started doing it regularly but found that they began feeling more and more isolated from the people they normally socialized with since they were certain they were the only ones in their "crowd" who smoked marijuana. Parties where everyone got drunk were no longer enjoyable, were in fact repulsive. Their old friends began to wonder why they never socialized any more, and Donnie and Charlene, basically sociable people, became very unhappy.

"You know, if you smoke grass," said Donnie, "you kinda start seeing things differently, and it's hard to have a good time with people who don't smoke. We want to turn our friends on, but I think if I bring it up to anyone, they'll call the cops."

Charlene giggled. "My brother's a cop. But what we've been doing lately is getting our friends high with nitrous oxide. We buy a tank of it, put some in a balloon, and then let people breathe it in from the balloon. That way you can't OD and it's legal!" She giggled again. "My brother comes over two or three times a week, after work and asks us for some laughing gas."

Jamie and I looked at each other again in astonishment.

Donnie continued, "We're hoping we can get our friends used to getting high, and then maybe we can turn them on to pot. It would be nice to have good times with our friends without getting drunk or feeling left out. It's weird how something like smoking or not smoking pot can separate you from your friends."

Donnie bought a ring for Charlene and traded an ounce of prime weed for a bracelet.

"Good luck," said Jamie as they prepared to leave. "I hope you turn all your friends on and keep close and tight with them."

As they drove out of the campground, Jamie said, "Damn! If you saw those two in San Luis Obispo, you would never guess—how isolated and unhappy they are. I mean the guy says he makes five hundred grand a year, and they feel cut off from other people and can't do anything about it. All over pot!" He put on a minstrel show voice: "Whoooee! White folks sho is strange."

We began to refer to our journey as The Magical Mystery Tour." Each day was a new experience, new people, new breathtaking deserts. While driving across those landscapes Jamie would sometimes intone a Navajo chant: "Beauty before me, Beauty behind me, Beauty around me...." And he would gesture expansively at the world around him. "You know," he would say, "people are either on the bus or off the bus. If you're on the bus, you're on the move, going somewhere. If you're not on the bus, then you're waiting at the bus stop hoping for a bus to come by. All everybody wants is to be on the bus."

I had not had a dollar of my own for weeks, but not once in that time had I worried about money. And Jill and Carol were pretty much forgotten. But always the bus was headed toward Phoenix, and as we got closer, Jamie would talk more of Sharon and their impending reunion, and less and less about The Magical Mystery Tour.

Gradually the understanding that the trip was coming to an end began to sink into my consciousness. Sometimes I wanted to grab Jamie and say, "How can you give up this freedom? Forget Sharon. She cheated on you with one of your best friends. Just stay on the bus. We could ride the bus forever, all over the country and into Mexico, trading jewelry, always surrounded by beauty. We could become underground legends, the magical hippies driving in and out of people's lives." With no commitments, no wives, no expectations.

But Jamie was cutting himself off from the journey. More and more of his thoughts were in Phoenix and the prospect of restarting his marriage. It was late October when we got there. Sharon was as beautiful as Jamie had indicated, but she and I didn't hit it off. There was nothing too obvious, just a coolness that we couldn't overcome. I tried as much as possible to stay out of their way. I continued sleeping in the bus parked in the driveway of Jamie's house and hung out there while Jamie and Sharon were doing a lot of talking in the house. At the end of two days, Jamie told me he and Sharon had agreed to stay together and try to work out their differences.

"I know it's going to be hard, but shit, man, we don't like living apart. We want to be with each other. I think I can change, and she's promised to be more open about what she wants and needs. We can do it."

I realized I couldn't stay with Jamie anymore and was once again on my own. There was a touch of panic as this realization set in. I was still broke and homeless, and New Mexico and San Francisco were a long way off. Where would I go?

"OK," I said. I guess I'll be on my way tomorrow."

"You going back to San Francisco?"

"I dunno. I think I'll hitch back to New Mexico."

"Aw no, man. You don't need to hitchhike. I'll pay for a bus ticket to Albuquerque, if that's where you wanna go."

So the next morning I caught a Greyhound bus to Albuquerque and spent the day watching the landscape through the window—Flagstaff, Gallup, Grants, and down into Albuquerque. Sitting in the bus I felt that I had cut loose of everyone and everything in La Perla, and now I doubted I would go back there, at least not for a long time. I wasn't sure where I would go, but that would be my next goal: figuring out where.

It was evening when I got to Albuquerque, so I called a friend who put me up for the night. Next day I hitchhiked south to see Kyle, a friend who was renting a farmhouse about forty miles north of La Perla. I stayed there for three days, and on the morning of the fourth day I followed an impulse and got on the road heading south to La Perla.

I got into town in the early afternoon, almost two months after I left, and went straight to Louie's house. Louie hugged me and offered his floor space and a bedroll to sleep in as long as I wanted. I was home.

"Tommy came back a few days after you left," said Louie, "so Jill moved out and is renting a house over by Bernardo Romero's place. Some guy in Las Cruses owns it. It's been empty for quite a while, so it was kinda trashed out. She's been fixing it up and is living in it now."

I suddenly felt that within minutes of my return it was as if the past two months had never happened. I guess as long as we both are in La Perla people will assume we're a couple. I'll ignore what they think. Soon they'll see that I'm not attached to anyone. I'm just accountable to me.

Feeling irritated, I walked over to Jill's new house. She was mud-plastering one of the rooms when I entered. She gave a shout and ran and hugged me tightly, her head nuzzling against my chest.

I told her of my experiences, not mentioning Carol, and she told me how much she had missed me. She invited me to dinner that night, so I spent the rest of the afternoon with her helping her plaster.

After that I thought of myself as living in Louie's house, even though most nights I spent with Jill. In the daytime I helped her work on her house, though I tried to keep it clear in my mind that I didn't live there. But somehow, slowly, it seemed that Jill and I had gotten together again. And again, I was not quite sure how that had happened, but psychologically, at any rate, I was still unattached.

Sometime later I got a letter from Carol addressed to me, care of Louie Caputti, General Delivery, La Perla. Was I there? How come I had not written to her? Could I have forgotten her so soon? Was I coming back to San Francisco?

San Francisco! That seemed like a lifetime ago. There really was a woman named Carol, and I had lived with her in San Francisco. And there really had been a Magical Mystery Tour. Why had we ever gotten off the bus? I tried to write to Carol but couldn't think of anything to say. Her next letter, about two weeks later, was petulant and angry, and I felt lucky to have left. I made no pretense at attempting to write back to her.

I continued living at Louie's, sleeping at Jill's—an arrangement that seemed satisfactory to everyone. Jill and I made few plans for the future, and we almost never again talked of building a community.

Louie's house   Photo by Geri Rhodes and Bob Christensen

Homebuilding

I was seated at the kitchen table reading Carlos Castaneda's *A Separate Reality* while I waited for the pot of water on the wood stove to boil for coffee when Louie walked in. He greeted me and sat down to wait for the coffee.

"Listen," I said, "I've been in La Perla for ten months, staying with you most of the time, and I've been thinking about having my own home. I've come up with an idea. I wanna see what you think of it."

"You can stay here as long as you need. There's no big hurry for you to move out."

"Thanks man. You've been great about letting me stay here, but I really want my own place. Here's what I'm thinking. Suppose I fix up the old stable in back here and move into it. I could put in some doors and windows, patch up the holes in the walls, and put in a floor. I could turn it into a nice place to live."

The water was boiling now and I started brewing the coffee. Louie was silent for a moment. "That's gonna take a lot of materials. How you gonna get wood and doors and stuff? Will you get a job to pay for them?"

Jamie had given me some money from our last jewelry sale and the change when he bought my bus ticket, but it was not nearly enough to cover the cost of everything I would need in order to turn the stable into a home. I had no desire to go back to the city and get a job—returning to the city to live, even for a few months, was unthinkable. But no matter how far from the city you try to go, you always need money sooner or later, and the city is the money place. How to get out of this bind?

Soon after this conversation, Louie and I stopped for a beer at the Willow Inn, a hanging-on-by-its-fingernails bar a few miles south of Sabinal. Its continued existence depended on the patronage of the farmers and freaks scattered throughout the valley which, considering the sparseness of that population base and its general lack of money, was not much. We got into a conversation with one of the local farmers who was cooling down from his field labors with a cold beer. He had just bought some acreage with an abandoned house on it and was looking for someone to demolish the structure. We agreed that I would raze the house in exchange for all the lumber, windows, and doors I needed and any other materials I could salvage.

The next day, with the help of freaks from La Perla, the demolition began. Soon we were hauling out truckloads of materials. With a hardworking crew, it took only a few days to tear the house down to the ground. There were not only enough lumber, windows and doors to fit my needs, but even after trips to the dump with stuff that was not usable, there was much material left over for any freak in La Perla who was doing remodeling or building. All the demolition cost me was my sweat, time, and the gas to haul the materials to La Perla.

And so it happened. I ended up with several good doors and windows and piles of lumber, from 1 x 2s to 2 x 8s. It took another week to remove all the nails from the lumber, and I was ready to start.

Louie had been using the stable as a storage space for all sorts of things, most of it suitable only for hauling to the dump. Once I had cleared it out, I began the actual rebuilding. The interior was one large room, twenty-five feet wide and forty-five feet long with a dirt floor hard-packed by horses' hooves over the years and a front entrance big enough for a wagon or a truck to drive through. Since it had been built as a stable, there were no windows. Fortunately, the roof was in surprisingly good shape. Like most buildings in La Perla, it was a flat roof consisting of planks covered with tar paper and a layer of dirt some six to eight inches thick on top of that. The dirt insulated the roof and, theoretically, kept the roof from leaking. If the roof of an adobe building leaks, water will erode the walls until they collapse. But this roof still had plenty of dirt, and there were only a few places where small leaks in the roof had caused holes in the walls near the top, where the *vigas* (the roof beams) rested on the top of the walls. The basic structure was sound; it just needed a lot of work to turn into a home.

The first thing I did to fix the leaks was lay more dirt up on the roof, hauling it up a ladder bucket by bucket. Hard, muscle-clenching work. After adding several inches to the existing layer of dirt, I leveled it so that it drained to the rear of the building and off through the *canales*, the gutter spouts that poured the water off the roof. Now the roof was water-tight and there would be no more damage to the walls should it rain.

When done carefully, and maintained regularly, this type of roof works very well, and keeps a house water-tight. If, however, it should rain for, say, three consecutive days, you will have a problem. The dirt on the roof gets saturated, and leaks spring up inside the house. In that case, there is nothing to do but place pans and buckets to catch the dripping water. After the rain stops and the sun dries the roof, your house is water-tight again. But how often does it rain for three consecutive days in the desert Southwest anyway?

Next, I repaired the holes along the top of the walls, filling them in with broken adobes, which were plentiful in La Perla, cutting and shaping them so that they fit into the holes, and using mud for mortar to seal them in place. Using a blade from a firewood bowsaw, I sawed through the adobe blocks which ringed the holes, turning the ragged edges of the holes into straight lines, squaring them up. Using the same blade, I cut good adobe blocks into sizes that fit tightly into the holes. I then mixed a few shovelfuls of dirt I dug from outside the door with a little water to make a nice thick mud. I applied the mud to the joints of the adobe blocks, and *voila!* the holes were fixed! Try doing that with any building material other than adobe.

This work of transformation was hard and satisfying. *Mud! Building a home out of mud!* A concept that still thrills me as I sit and write today in my current adobe home.

The first cities in the world were made of mud, and I felt a connection over the millennia with a homeowner in ancient Sumer or Ur of the Chaldees sweating under the Biblical sun as he weatherized his home, a never-ending task with adobe structures. Perhaps he was my avatar, or I his reincarnation. It was exhilarating to be a link in a chain extending back to civilization in its infancy. I personally may have been transient, but what I was doing was eternal. I was a bridge spanning the distant past and the budding future.

After fixing the holes in the walls, I installed doors and windows to let in light and keep out the weather. One of the benefits of adobe homes is that you can use a hacksaw blade to cut out a hole in the six-inch thick wall for a door or window, and then cut out a space for a beam to insert as a lintel above the door or window to keep it from collapsing. I cut holes in the walls for a back door and for three windows. After inserting the windows and hanging the rear door, I nailed planks from the ground to the ceiling, closing off the wide opening in front and narrowing it to a standard door size, and hung a door there. My space was now enclosed and out of the weather. It was becoming quite cozy.

Good Dog

One bright April morning a large, black and white, wooly-haired dog appeared at my door. He was discrete and deferential, asking for nothing more than a bite to eat and a sip of water. As he ate I sat outside and talked with him while he listened intently and responded with an occasional tail wag or side-wise glance at me. By the time he was through eating, we were buddies.

I took him in and named him for what he was, Good Dog. We became constant companions and went everywhere together, visiting friends scattered throughout the little community, walking in the desert, or just lying quietly at home. It was my practice at this time in my life to ingest LSD once a week and walk up on the mesa to experience the desert, which spread out for miles to the east until it reached the foothills of the mountains thirty miles away. I could walk out my back door, head south, and in ten minutes I was out of sight of the entire town. A one hour walk put me in a solitary desert where the only indication that humans had ever been there were the dim outlines of the foundations of structures built by the Piro Indians before the coming of the Spaniards.

I would walk out not so much to *think* about life as to *feel* it under the influence of the LSD. (I sometimes wonder how different civilization would be if Descartes had said "I *feel* therefore I am.") Good Dog was my only companion on these excursions. Like me, he had the ability to make himself invisible on these jaunts. I would take off all my clothes, and we would sit motionless, not talking for hours, protected from the broiling sun by the sparse shade of a mesquite tree, watching the desert life as it continued its business all around us. The beetles trekked across the broad expanse of desert in a line of march that was undeviating and obviously purposeful. The birds chattered excitedly in the mesquite trees and chaparral, passing on the news of the day, always keeping one eye on us. The lizards scurried about like waiters in coat and tails, busy, busy, busy. And the rabbits hung out beneath the rabbit bush, gossiping, twitching their noses, giggling, and nibbling constantly. I would sit as immobile as stone while Good Dog sat beside me, only his dark eyes moving, watching everything. After several hours we would rise and return home, discussing what we had seen that day, trying to decipher what it all meant.

It was while walking back from one of these excursions that Good Dog taught me one of his teachings.

"All things," he said, "are moving; nothing stands still. All creatures move along their own particular lines: Dogs move on dog lines, humans on human lines; no-legs, two-legs, four-legs, everything travels along the line set for it. And everything wants to move from simple to complex, but not all succeed." He paused and looked at me with a grin. "*Evolution* you call it. Other creatures don't have a name for it; they just know that's the way things are. But not everyone is moving up, from simple to complex. Some are going the other way, from complex to simple. Everything wants to move up, but some have finished their upward journey, and they come down.

"Consider," he continued, "that all things begin by moving up, but then they reach their peak and start moving down. Creatures that are moving up eventually learn to reason and think, to remember. When they reach that point, they start explaining, they think about *Why* and they forget to pay attention to *What*. They invent religion, God, and meaning. We dogs make dog religions, horses make horse religions, and though our gods are quite different, they are also basically the same. This is a paradox of life."

He stopped, cocked his right ear and looked at me, quizzical and sly. "Think now, as we dogs make our dog religion, what role does Man play in the mythology of dogs? What do you think? Is he demon or angel?"

We stood looking across the desert. He spoke again. "It all depends on which way a being is moving, up or down on the evolution escalator. Some creatures are simply mistakes and never move up, only down. Yeah, God makes mistakes. Gods too are moving up or down on the escalator.

"Has Man reached the top of the escalator? Has he peaked out? Once a being peaks out, there is no way to go but down. Eventually it degenerates until it becomes a fleck of protoplasm floating on the breeze or in the sea, so small that nobody can see it, no one can tell if it is still alive. It stays there until it begins the journey up again, maybe further up, maybe not so far.

"In dog mythology you'll either be my god or my devil, all creatures' god or devil, depending on how you humans behave toward life in all its forms. Your behavior toward us nonhumans indicates whether you're moving up or down the escalator of existence."

He grinned at me, his tongue lolling in the heat. "So," he asked again, what do you think? Will you be my god or a devil?" He started trotting back to La Perla.

I was too ashamed and embarrassed to say what I thought.

Good Dog taught me that every day is different from the day before, that every trip into the desert was new, even if we always walked the same path to the same place. There was always something new to experience, to smell, to hear, to see. He taught me that the world moves in cycles, but that being in a cycle is not the same as being in a rut. Every day the sun rises in the east, forever, but every day is new.

He taught me that there is no such thing as a steady, stable world. The world is fluid, in constant flux, and how you perceive it is not determined by its actual *reality*, but by your sensory apparatus. His perception of the world was completely different from mine. Walking in the desert, he would pause and concentrate on an odor in the breeze. "Do you smell that?" he would ask.

I would try to pick up the smell, and get nothing.

"Concentrate, concentrate. Don't drift away. Pay attention to the world around you."

He would stop at a pile of scat and sniff. "Coyote was by here yesterday. Last meal he had was a rabbit. Walked off that way, toward the east. He stopped here and picked up our scent from last week. Probably watching us right now from that rise over there."

Suddenly I was aware that our weekly excursions were not just about us and what we saw; the whole desert was teeming with life observing *us*, all sorts of creatures, seen and unseen, watching and judging everything we did. "God or devil?"

With Good Dog, not only was the desert much more alive and mysterious, life itself was. But his final lesson about life was the hardest. He taught me how to die.

One morning he dragged himself home, weak and bleeding. He had been attacked by a pack of coyotes. Somehow he managed to escape them, still alive but just barely. His throat was ripped, and when I gave him water, I could see water running out through the punctures. I tried disinfecting the wounds but there was no way that he could eat or drink, and he had lost so much blood he could no longer stand. He had come home to die.

Good Dog was totally accepting of his impending death. He had come back because he wanted to die at home, not because he thought he could escape his death. Now, lying in my arms, he seemed at peace.

"Why are you so damned upset?" he asked. "Did you think

I would live forever? Do you think *you* will live forever? Everything dies. I just want you to make my death faster, easier. You must help me end it now. Borrow Len's gun. You know what you must do."

"No."

"Don't be foolish and sentimental. Do it. You have to help me die."

"No. I can't do that."

He managed to turn his head and look at me. "Do it," he said. "Do it now."

Confrontation

My y next project was to put in a wooden floor over the dirt. I was working on this, down on my knees nailing in boards one day when I noticed a slight swelling on my right side, about half way down my rib cage. It was a little tender when I touched it, but not really painful. The swelling was a bit disturbing, but it did not seem particularly serious. I decided to go to the doctor and get it checked when I had the free time and a ride to town. But something weird began to happen.

A few days after I first noticed this growth, the area around it became increasingly tender and painful. Soon my entire right side and part of my back were in constant pain, but the worse the pain got, the less inclined I was to go to the doctor. I had recently read Castaneda's *Teachings of Don Juan* and was still reading *A Separate Reality*. Both books deal with the teachings of a Mexican Yaqui Indian shaman, *Don* Juan Matus, as conveyed to Castaneda, an anthropologist from the University of Southern California whom *Don* Juan had taken on as his "apprentice" shaman. *Don* Juan counsels Castaneda that "Death is your best advisor." Death follows you wherever you go, right behind you, by your left shoulder. When making important decisions, you should always consult Death, and let Death guide you to the proper course of action. With Death as advisor, silliness and foolishness become impossible.

I had come to La Perla looking for something, but I had not yet been able to determine exactly what it was I was looking for.

For as long as I could remember, what I did with my life was in response to obligations and responsibilities that were not really mine by choice but were imposed on me from the outside by others' expectations of me and by the social and economic system we live in—the need for a job and the need "to make a living," which really meant nothing more than making money. I knew that part of the reason for my being in La Perla was to get away from these imposed requirements, to find out who and what I was when freed from them. I truly felt that I could achieve this freedom, and once free I would acquire an understanding that would permit me to live my life in a meaningful, enlightened way. But I had not yet been able to eliminate the trivial and foolish from my life. My ego's need for praise and security still seemed to be the motivating force in my behavior. It was my ego, not death, that was always beside me. I got upset if I felt people were not treating me in accordance with my true worth, especially women. But there was so much about myself that I didn't know or understand. I often felt like a case of arrested adolescence. (Tommy once referred to me as "an eternal fourteen-year old." I think he meant it as praise, but it was too close to truth, and my feelings were hurt. My ego again.) I concluded that it was time to consult my death, to clear out the nonsense, and be left only with that which really matters, no matter what it was.

I began to think of the growth on my side and its accompanying pain as a manifestation of my death. I reasoned that if the tumor were malignant, there would be a point beyond which its effects would be irreversible, and my death would ensue. I would gamble on where that point was by doing nothing about the tumor, letting the growth and pain run their course, and then when I had flushed the trivial out of my life, I would go to the doctor and determine if I was too late to halt its progress. If not, I could recover and live my life as a truly changed person. If it was too late, I would die, but at least I would die with an awakened consciousness and my death would be meaningful to me. I decided to take the gamble.

As the pain spread and intensified, I was constantly aware of this growth, and I began to accept my death as a real possibility. I told no one and continued doing my usual tasks, spending most of my time working on my home. But there was no enlightenment, no burst of light, no new understanding. So I waited and waited.

Even though I told no one, I'm sure the experience was affecting my behavior. One night I was sleeping at Jill's when she woke from a nightmare screaming. When she saw me lying beside her she grabbed me and held me. She dreamed she had walked into a room that was empty, except for a bed with a body on it, covered by a sheet. She pulled back the sheet and saw me lying there with my eyes closed. I opened them and said, "Jill, I'm dying." At that point she awoke.

One day in October, about a month after I first discovered the tumor, I was working on the flooring of my house, and when I bent down to pick up my hammer I had a sudden and excruciating pain in my chest. I fell to the floor clutching at my heart. But even as this was happening, I was certain that this was not a pain to be frightened of, that it was not a stroke or coronary. I remained calm, sitting on the floor leaning against the wall. In a few moments the pain was gone, and I resumed working.

That evening my elderly neighbor, *Don* Genaro, came to tell me that there had been a phone call from my father, an emergency involving my mother. I went to his house fully expecting to hear the worst about my mother. When my father answered the phone, he told me that my oldest brother had died of a stroke. The shock was overwhelming. I had an instant vision of my brother as my protector, he being the oldest and I the youngest. He always made sure that I was treated fairly and equally by the other, older kids we played with, threatening to fight the others if they did not include me in their play. I stood holding the phone, literally incapable of speech, able only to groan and gasp incomprehensibly. Death had come, only not for me.

I caught a bus to Phoenix that afternoon and have no memory whatsoever of that ride. I remember only the feeling that I was drowning in a sea of death. I had lived with Death for over a month, and now my brother's death was staking a place beside mine. Death was everywhere. This feeling was intensified when I found out that my brother had died at the time that I had felt the pain in my chest while working on my house.

During my stay at my folks' house in Phoenix I slept on the living room floor while my brother from California slept on the couch. On our last night there, he questioned my life.

"What are you doing living in that place in New Mexico?"

"What do you mean?"

"You should be doing something with your life instead of running away and hiding out with a bunch of do-nothing hippies."

"You don't know what I'm doing with my life."

"I know you quit teaching and you aren't working. You're just wasting your time, man. What do you do, get stoned and stand around looking at flowers all day saying 'Wow!'? That's a hell of a way to live your life. You're smart, you're educated, you could do something, be someone. Instead you run away and hide in the middle of nowhere in New Mexico."

"You don't know what you're talking about. I'm not running away from anything."

"Well, the folks won't tell you, but they're really hurt and disappointed at what you're doing. Taking all your education and turning into a nobody doing nothing. Jesus!"

"Shut up and let me sleep."

The conversation ended.

When I returned to Albuquerque I was confused over what I was doing, not only about the tumor on my side, but over my life in general. Was my brother right? Should I go back into the mainstream, get a job, get married again, have a family, and then what? I had tried that and had been unhappy to the point of madness. Or was I mad now? Was I any happier now than I had been when I was "a productive citizen?" Did I really know any more now about myself and how to live my life?

Those three days in Phoenix had been saturated with death. There was the wake and funeral, and all the talk of death that went with that. There was the constant pain in my side and my own preoccupation with death. Now death was all I thought about, and I was more confused than ever before. Certainly, my confrontation with death had brought no understanding, no new knowledge.

Upon returning to New Mexico, I hitched a ride to my friend Kyle's house, about forty miles north of La Perla. That evening, sitting on his front porch I revealed to him what had been happening to me. He was aghast.

"Go to a doctor," he said, "go right away. I'll take you to Albuquerque tomorrow to get checked."

"I can't do that," I argued. "I haven't learned anything from any of this. I'm the same ignorant person I've always been, and I do and worry about the same stupid things, still tangled up in my ego and trivia, all the same shit as always. But I still think *Don* Juan is right; once I accept Death as my advisor, I will clean up my life."

"You know what *Don* Juan would say about what you're doing? He'd say, 'That's a crappy way to die.'"

I refused to go to a doctor and headed back to La Perla. I needed someone else to talk to, to help me figure out what to do. I went to see Jill. She took one look at me and hugged me tight.

"My God. What happened to you in Phoenix? You look terrible. I guess I didn't realize how much your brother's death meant to you."

I started to explain about the tumor and *Don* Juan and Death. I was talking to her, sitting on the couch with my eyes closed, when a curtain of blackness started slowly falling down across the light coming through my eyelids, a blackness so thick it was tactile, I could *feel* it in my nose and mouth, blocking the passages like wads of cotton, shutting off my breath. As it dropped down, wiping out all traces of light, it was taking me with it, pushing me out of my mind into a place of terror and nothingness, obliterating everything, including my precious ego. I had stopped in mid-sentence and was no longer capable of talking or thinking. I was facing total oblivion and feeling a terror unlike anything I had ever felt before. I was slipping away into some otherwhere, and I knew I would never be able to find my way back. I knew *with certainty* that I was dying. I had reached where I thought I wanted to be, in confrontation with my death, and I was terrified as never before. There was *nothing*, no enlightenment, no understanding, no radiant light, nothing but absolute blackness and the absence of everything, including me.

And then dimly, from a great distance, I heard Jill's frightened voice calling to me. There was only a small speck of *me* left, and using what little strength I had, I grabbed on to her voice and used it to try to get back. I knew I was literally in a life and death struggle, and if I let go of her voice, I would never get back. I held onto that voice from so far away, clutching it, and pulled and pulled, and the voice got stronger and stronger, and then I was sitting on her couch, struggling to take a breath, to open my eyes. She was shaking me and shouting in my face.

"What's happening to you?!"

I didn't answer her question, just mumbled at her to hold me and not let go. For several minutes I just sat there enveloped in her embrace, shivering uncontrollably. I finally managed to respond.

"I don't know, I don't know. I think I was dying." The next day Jill drove me to a hospital in Albuquerque where I was tested and examined. The doctor probed the lump on my side, took a scalpel, sliced the skin and removed a lump of fatty tissue. "No problem. Totally benign," he said as he bandaged the shallow wound.

"But what about the pain that came with it?"

"Could be a coincidence. The pain might have been caused by something else. Have you been doing any physical labor that might have caused an injury, a pulled muscle, for example?"

"Yeah, I've been doing a lot of labor. I remember now that at one time I was bending over picking up a heavy plank, and I was kinda twisted and got a twinge in my side. But that just lasted a couple of minutes and was gone."

"Sometimes it takes several days for that kind of injury to become noticeable. And after the pain starts and you keep on working, you start adjusting what you do in response to it, and you no longer lift things naturally and make the injury worse. At any rate the tumor is no threat to your health. Take a few days rest, let your body heal and the pain should go away."

Suddenly my great endeavor, my tempting of death to acquire understanding, what I had secretly thought of as a noble act, changed to the ridiculous. I had become an actor in a farce. All I could do was grin at my foolishness.

Jill was sitting in the waiting room. She saw the smile on my face and jumped up and hugged me. "You're ok!"

"Yeah, my physical health is all right, but I may be a little nuts. Let's go home."

I rode back to La Perla in silence, reveling in the feeling of being healthy and alive. I looked at the cumulus clouds gathering above the majestic Sandia Mountains east of Albuquerque and the green ribbon of the *bosque* bordering the Rio Grande to the west. Beyond the river I could see the mesa rising toward the western horizon and several inactive volcanic craters on the gentle slope. The October sky was a crystalline sapphire blue. As we headed onto the Isleta Indian Reservation that borders the city to the south I looked over at Jill driving her van in silence.

My God! It's so beautiful! Magical! Everything works as it should, everything fits together in one piece, including me. I'm a part of this beauty. What I've been looking for is all around me. Don Juan was right: Death is everywhere, but that's only because Life is everywhere. Of course! It isn't death I've been looking for, it's life. Confronting my death has taught me something. It just isn't what I expected. The journey begins with acceptance, not understanding. I just have to accept who I am where I am. It's merely the beginning, but who knows? Maybe understanding will come later.

Jill glanced at me and saw me looking at her. She smiled.

"You know," I said, "I've been kinda crazy for a while. I've been wallowing in death, but I'm out of it now. It's really great just to be with you riding in this car on this beautiful day. Now I just want to get back to La Perla and be alive with my friends. And I've still got a home to finish building."

Homebuilding II

Life in La Perla continued swirling around me as I worked my way through the maze of building a home. I was an academic, not a construction person. Although my father worked in construction and tried to teach me about it, I am ashamed to admit that when I was younger I looked down on people who labored for a living, including my father, so I did my damnedest not to learn. Now that I had grown to respect my father greatly, to see him as a role model, I was kicking myself mentally for my youthful stupidity. I had many missteps, dead-ends, and start-overs. To my surprise, building a home was as much mental work as it was physical labor. I was ignorant about so many things, but ignorance was something I could cure by doing, so I jumped into the work without really knowing *what* I was doing. I can't claim that the home I was building was a paragon of construction, but it was *mine*, a product of my thought and sweat, and as with any parent looking at his child, it was beautiful.

I can describe the building of my home, but what is almost inexpressible is the joy that came with the labor. *I was making, building, creating my home!* I had never imagined I could do something like that. Such a basic activity—nesting—was not part of my experience. In La Perla, most if not all of the houses were built by the people who lived in them. When that's true, the house and the land it stands on become part of you.

Every day I couldn't wait to get started. I arose at daybreak, ate, and then went to work. The days were never long enough to do everything I wanted to do. And that too is a good feeling. I completed the floor in a couple of weeks and then I could concentrate on niceties. Hey, this was my home and I could put whatever niceties I desired in it. I had recently bought a box of colored glass panes, square ones four inches on a side and round ones four inches in diameter. I cut holes high in the east wall of my home, inserted the colored glass into the adobes about one to two feet below the ceiling, and sealed them off with mud. Every morning the sun would splash in pools of different colored light through the wall and into the room.

I then punched a hole five feet high in one of the walls, pushed a stove pipe through it, put an elbow on the outside pointing up and ran the pipe up so that the end was higher than the roof. Otherwise the stove pipe would not draw the smoke out. On the inside, I put an elbow pointing down so that the pipe connected to my wood stove. Now I could have heat in the late fall and winter, and boil water for coffee. Warm and snug as every home should be.

Next, I dug a pit three feet deep at the north end of my home, and built a platform four feet high above it. The platform was my bed, and the pit beneath it was storage space. Warm weather was ending as were my labors on my house. I used a wire brush to round off edges of the bare adobes on the inside walls, and then plastered the walls with mud plaster, not with a trowel, but with my hand so that I could follow the contours of the adobes. I then mixed up some whitewash and, using the biggest brush I could get (a push broom), whitewashed the interior walls. The room became light and bright. The effects of whitewash are different from the effects of paint, almost like a liquid stucco with a warm white glow. Whitewash and adobe were made for each other.

My home was completed by the time the weather turned cold. It's true that I had no running water, but Louie, just thirty yards away, did have indoor plumbing where I got my water. Nor did I have electricity, but the house was bright in sunlight, and at night my kerosene lanterns gave a soft, almost mysterious glow. My home was simplicity itself, but for me, it was comfort in the extreme.

People enjoyed my home, and often came to visit. When the freaks in La Perla decided to have a music night every Friday ("If you don't play an instrument, bring pots and pans you can beat on."), my home was selected as the place to congregate. Soon word of music night spread throughout the various freak communities, and those people started coming, many bringing their kids who beat on pots with great enthusiasm. I remember my home packed with people and whirling, spinning energy and sound, which to us was music. My home! I had never felt so much at home in my life.

Roof with stove pipe   Photo courtesy of Bob Christensen

Working on the Well

In early December I had finished my house. I installed a wood-burning heating stove, put in several kerosene lanterns, and I was done. I was snug and cozy now in my own space where I could be alone whenever I felt the need for solitude.

Now too I began another project: preparing for a garden. Cash was always a scarcity in La Perla. None of the freaks in La Perla were on food stamps (one of the few decisions we made as a group: To take food stamps would be hypocritical since we wanted to free ourselves as much as possible from the "gummint"), so in order to have enough to eat, we had to supplement our incomes by growing gardens large enough to supply much of our food during the summer. However, the rainfall in south central New Mexico is not enough to grow crops without irrigation, and the irrigation ditches in La Perla had been closed down for years from lack of use.

All the homes had running water for domestic use, but the water system was notoriously unreliable. The pump that had been installed years before to supply water for the school had been converted to public use when the school was closed down. Everyone connected onto the school water line and used the school pump. I never knew who or if anyone paid the electrical bill for the pump. The resulting water system was a maze of rusting one-inch iron pipe that ruptured periodically, and when it did, the water flow to each house slowed to a trickle. Then the people would walk the water lines looking for the leak by searching for the wet spot created by the seepage. The line would be dug up, the rusted section removed, a new section added, and then the line buried again. Obviously one could not rely on the existing water system to grow a garden.

The solution to the water problem was to sink your own irrigation well. La Perla was level with the Rio Grande a few hundred yards away, so the water table was shallow, some twenty feet below the surface. At thirty-five feet there was an abundance of water. It wasn't, however, good enough to drink—for potable water you needed a well about one-hundred fifty feet deep—but a shallow well was suitable for irrigating a garden. Since money was scarce we could not pay a well-digger, and people who wanted a garden to help get them through the year had to sink their own well.

Before I began working on my well I had put a fence around the garden area to keep out the cows and sheep which roamed free throughout La Perla. For the post-and-rail fence I had cut large branches from dead cottonwoods and attached them to creosote-treated posts I sunk in the ground. Now I was ready to do my well.

To sink my well I used seven sections of five-foot long, two-inch diameter pipe, seven couplings, and a sand point. Each section of pipe was threaded at both ends, and seven sections could be coupled to make one thirty-five-foot length of pipe. The sand point is a three-foot section of pipe that comes to a point, like a nail. One end of the sand point is threaded and can be connected to a five-foot section; the pointed end is slotted, with a fine screen mesh covering the slots which run about half the length of the point. The water table is water-saturated sand, not an underground lake, and the sand point lets water through while filtering out the sand. Over a period of years, the screen gets clogged up by calcium deposits, and the pipe must be pulled up, the sand point replaced, and a new well sunk.

When I sank my irrigation well, I first dug a pit, six by six and eight feet deep, located in the middle of where my garden was to be. The pit would serve several functions. A water pump *pushes* water more efficiently than it sucks it up. The water would be sucked up to the bottom of the pit, and then pushed up the last eight feet. So by placing the pump underground, you made the pump work more efficiently. Being underground also prevented the water in the pipe and pump from freezing. I dug stairs from the surface down to the bottom of the pit where the pump was. On the surface, the pit opening was covered by planks with a hole in the middle where the water pipe stuck out and was connected to a large hose that could reach anywhere in the garden.

Digging the pit was a meditation in itself. Slowly I went down through the varied strata of the earth, going backward through time, through topsoil, sand, caliche, rock. At one point, *two feet beneath the surface*, I found an old Chinese coin, a round coin with a square hole in the middle. Two feet beneath the surface? What mystery brought it there and when? As I went deeper, six, seven feet, I found roots that would break through the walls of my pit during the night, some mere filaments, others thick as my little finger. The nearest tree was a cottonwood, some fifty feet to the south, but there were tree roots breaking through from all directions. All other trees were at least several hundred feet away. Sometimes a root tip would peek through the wall, and the next day there would be a tiny bud of a leaf forming, and in a few days there would be a full-blown leaf sticking out of the dirt seven feet deep, twisting blindly toward the sun above. By the time I finished digging, the four walls were furred and burred by roots and leaves of varied types and sizes. *The Earth really is alive.* Not just metaphorically, not just on the surface, but all of it, everywhere, an interlocking mesh of life. Here I was, tapping into water flowing through sand thirty-five feet below the topsoil; who knows what life that river supported underground as well as the life it supported on the surface. Here were the roots of plants, eight feet down, twisting and turning like blind worms in the light, roots that became leaves starving for life, for sunshine, avid to achieve their potentiality, to become the shoot, the bud, the bloom, and then back to the seed.

After the pit was dug, I placed two beams across the top of the pit and began the actual process of sinking the well. I took two coupled sections of pipe with the sand point attached to one end and lowered the pipe until the sand point rested on the bottom of the pit. Now I had what looked like a giant nail, about thirteen feet long, with five feet of pipe sticking up above the surface. With some help from my friends and the use of a pile driver, I started sinking the sand point and pipe into the ground.

It took two people to work the pile driver. The driver was a thick iron sleeve about four feet long, open at one end, that slipped over the end of the pipe. The other end of the driver was closed, and the sleeve at that point was filled with twelve inches of lead for additional weight. It had two handles for the operators to hold on to. The whole unit weighed about seventy-five pounds. Two people facing each other would each grab one of the handles, lift the driver until it barely covered the top of the pipe, and then slam it down with all the force they could muster. The sand point would pierce the ground and go down a few inches. The operation would be repeated. And repeated. Each time the pipe would go down a few inches. If the ground were hard, the pipe might go down one inch or less. When the pipe had gone down far enough, another section of pipe would be coupled to it, and the process repeated.

Maybe one very strong person could do the job by himself, but it was hard enough with two—sweaty work made easier with friends. They would stop by and work on the pile driver for a while. There was nothing in it for them, especially if they already had a well of their own, but we had the unstated understanding that without cooperation there could be no community. And in that sense alone, the hard work was very satisfying.

After the pipe had been sunk far enough, which took about a week, one end of the water pump would be attached to the pipe at the bottom of the pit, and the other end to the last section which ran up to the top. If you were unlucky, you might sink a pipe fifteen, sixteen feet and hit a large rock underground and not be able to go any farther. In that case, you had to pull the pipe out (a job in itself), move the well to another location, and start again.

Obviously, sinking a well was not a project that was undertaken lightly. It entailed the investment of what was for us of a huge amount of money and required much time and hard work. But more importantly, it was a commitment to one's place, a way of saying "I'm here to stay." Once a well was sunk, it was much harder to pull up stakes and leave.

After I made the electrical connections to my pump and pulled the switch, the pump started humming, and a few moments later water came gushing out the pipe. At that moment I felt that I was in the presence of something mysterious, almost magical. Not just the exciting fact that I was getting water from the bowels of the Earth, but also what that water meant and represented. I had become part of a cycle that everyone knows and takes for granted, but which no one truly understands: the cycle of water and the existence of life. It's so simple. You stick a seed in the ground, provide it with water, and a plant grows. You eat the plant, and the ingested plant becomes part of you and gives you the life and energy to stick another seed in the ground. What could be simpler? And yet, what is more mysterious and incomprehensible? We can put labels and names on the process—chlorophyll, light, photosynthesis, blah blah—and think thereby that we know how it happens, but in fact all we've done is label. The process itself remains shrouded in mystery. No one can tell me how water can combine with a seed the size of a flea and produce a plant heavy with tomatoes, or how that tomato is eaten and becomes *me*. Sinking a well and growing a garden (the first garden

I ever grew) made me feel a part of something immeasurably greater than I was.

But not everyone's attempts at well-making were successful. You understood from the beginning that you might wind up losing all your time and money.

Joel started sinking his well several months after I had finished mine. He too dug a pit and started the pile-driving. I went over one morning to help him. Joel and friends had already driven in about fifteen feet of pipe during the previous two days. The two of us took the pile driver and started banging the pipe in deeper. It was mid-June and about one hundred degrees.

We worked silently, except for the grunt each time we slammed the pile-driver. After a couple of hours we had gone down another five feet, and then the pipe stopped going down. No matter how hard or how many times we slammed down the piledriver, the pipe did not budge. We banged the driver until we were gasping for breath and our eyes were stinging with the sweat that ran into them. The pipe did not move. With arms aching, we decided to smoke a joint and consider what we could do.

We concluded that we had hit a large rock and would have to pull up the pipe and change the location of the well at the bottom of the pit. We fervently hoped we had not hit an extensive layer of rock, instead of just a boulder.

We went to Genaro Calderon who had once worked for the railroad and borrowed a gigantic jack, one used to lift railroad cars. We wrapped a chain around the pipe sticking out of the ground and hooked it to the jack. Joel pumped the jack, the chain became taut, the pipe jerked, and then began coming up. When we pulled the pipe out of the ground, we saw that the sand point had snapped off the pipe and was now some twenty feet below ground.

So Joel went to Socorro the next day and bought another sand point. We picked a location at the bottom of the pit as far from the first attempt as we could get. We worked all morning and halfway through the afternoon. We had gone down some ten feet when the pipe stopped moving. Once again we kept slamming the pile-driver, and once again the pipe did not budge.

Another joint and another discussion. We came to a painful decision. We would have to pull up the pipe, dig another pit in the yard, and start all over again. Once again we wrapped a chain around the pipe, attached it to the jack, and started pumping the jack. The jack was sitting over the pipe, resting on two massive beams, eight by eight, ten feet long. Joel pumped the jack and the chain became more and more taut until the two beams began to bow under the tremendous pressure exerted by the jack. The pipe did not move, not a fraction of an inch.

Another discussion. We decided that I would go into the pit with a large pipe wrench, and I would twist the pipe while Joel worked the jack. Perhaps then we could break the pipe loose from whatever demonic force was holding it. And so it was done. As I pulled on the pipe wrench with all my force, the super-taut chain was about a foot from my face. It was then that I noticed that one of the links of the chain was actually broken—it was no longer an oval, but a hook connected to the links on either end. I removed the wrench and stepped back.

"What's the matter?" asked Joel.

"Oh, I was just remembering an old saying I never really understood until now."

"What?"

"A chain is as strong as its weakest link." I pointed to the broken link. "Do you realize what would happen to me or you if that chain broke?"

"Oh Jesus! It would burst your head like a watermelon."

"Or snap off your legs."

For the first time since I had been helping Joel with his well he looked depressed rather than angry and frustrated.

"Fuck it! Get out of there."

We released the jack, removed the chain, went inside and smoked a joint.

"I guess I'm not supposed to have a well."

This was a disturbing comment to make. Without the well the amount of food one could grow in the garden was severely restricted. It also had implications of a reduced commitment to his place.

"I'll help you dig a pit and sink another well somewhere else in your yard."

"No. The message is clear. No well."

I was shocked. Joel was not a person to give up or admit defeat easily. Now he was sitting looking glumly at the huge hole in his yard with a section of pipe sticking out.

"I can't grow enough food just using the school water line.

It would take all day just to get a portion of the garden damp. I don't know. I don't know what I'm supposed to do now."

Both Joel and Sara were depressed for days afterward, which depressed me. They talked about going away for a while, making some money. And then Don Genaro died, the best friend the freaks had among the old timers. There was a pall over La Perla.

A couple weeks after Genaro died, Joel and Sara got part-time jobs in a natural foods restaurant in Albuquerque. He and Sara would spend a few days in Albuquerque, and then come to La Perla for a few days, and then head back to Albuquerque. Soon the periods spent in Albuquerque became longer than the time spent in La Perla. Joel had been the first freak to move to La Perla, and he and Sara were such an integral part of life there that it was almost impossible to visualize La Perla without them. The garden they had started dried and died, and the goat-heads and kochia took over the yard. Soon there was no indication that anything but weeds had ever grown there. And dominating the entire yard was collapsing hole with a three-inch pipe jutting out of it.

A Death

Genaro Calderon died on December 21st, the winter solstice, the day the sun completes one cycle and turns and begins a new one. He was eighty-two. He and his wife, Maria, lived next door to Louie and me. They lived alone since their children, like so many others from La Perla, had gone to fight in World War II, and those that returned after the War stayed only a few months and then left, usually to California. The children who had been too young to fight, left shortly after reaching adulthood. Now, once or twice a year, they came back for a few days to let the old folks get to know the grandkids and to talk about the old days in La Perla, before the War and jobs with the Santa Fe Railroad drained the town of all its youth.

Don Genaro—as a man of honor and dignity, *Don*, the Spanish title of respect, applied naturally to him—and Maria were friendly with all the freaks from the time the first ones, Joel, Tommy, and Louie, arrived and bought houses. They were not put off by these long-haired, bearded men they had suddenly acquired as neighbors. What they saw were young men working hard to renovate old houses and turn them back into homes.

"It's so good to see young people in La Perla again," said Maria. "These houses have been dead for a long time, and now they're coming back to life. It's like a little miracle."

But not all the old timers felt this way about the freaks. Some saw their arrival as an invasion by foreigners. For them we were a sign of the final deterioration of the community, the driving of the last coffin nail in the old way of life. Ironically, we freaks were trying, as much as we could, to get back to that older style of living.

Genaro suffered from gout, and some days was incapable of little more than sitting in a chair in pain. Maria was frail and suffered from the innumerable aches and illnesses that come with age. The freaks looked on them as surrogate parents, and we saw to it that their needs were always taken care of. We never went on a firewood run without getting enough wood for them and chopping it and stacking it neatly. If there was a leak in their roof, the freaks gathered and repaired it. Whenever we went to Socorro for groceries and supplies, we checked to see if they needed anything. When their children came to visit from California, they always made a point to seek out the freaks and thank them for watching over their parents.

On the morning of December 21st, Genaro awoke feeling poorly, so after a cup of coffee with milk and sugar and some toast, he went back to bed. When Maria looked in on him a while later, he was dead.

Everyone in La Perla was shocked at this unexpected death. Don Genaro was a good man who had no enemies, no one who in his secret self felt any joy at his demise. We freaks felt that we had lost a family member. Within two days the children and grandchildren began arriving, and the rental cars were lined up in front of the Calderon home. Arrangements for the funeral were made, and people kept arriving with plates of food for the guests so that Maria would not have to deal with feeding them.

Willie Sandoval, the town drunk and philosopher ("I'm a drinker and a thinker, a walker and a talker"), and a nephew from Belen requested and were granted the privilege of digging the grave with pick and shovel in the hard, rocky dirt in the town cemetery at the southeastern end of town. The day before the funeral, I could see them from my front window on this cold, grey day, methodically moving the rock and clay into a mound, making Don Genaro his final resting place. It took about four hours to get the hole just right. They shouldered their tools and reported to the family that the grave was ready.

The next day a requiem mass was celebrated in the Sacred Heart Church, on the opposite end of town from the cemetery. The priest, Father Frank, was a young Chicano dude from East L.A. I would see him walking in the *bosque* along the Rio Grande or up on the desert of the mesa wearing a mesh see-through muscle shirt and black bell-bottom pants. His parish included La Perla, Concepcion, Veguita, Las Nutrias, Sabinal, and *Bosque*. Nobody knew what terrible infraction Father Frank was guilty of that would have led the Church to exile him from L.A. to La Perla. There were rumors that he was actually a Zen Buddhist posing as a priest.

When Father Frank served mass on special occasions, such as Easter, or midnight mass on Christmas Eve, or a requiem, he was positively inspiring. He celebrated Don Genaro's mass in Spanish, and he was angelic, the embodiment of *living* ritual. When he raised his arms above his head holding the host and proclaimed the presence of the living Christ right there in that little church, everyone sighed audibly and we bowed our heads in a fervor of belief, even the unbelievers. When he called for our grief, we sobbed, and when he exhorted us to temper our grief with joy at Genaro's release, we turned and hugged each other.

The plain wooden coffin was carried down the aisle and down main street by sons and grandsons, led by Father Frank. The people from La Perla and the surrounding communities followed in procession, slowly, solemnly. The cortege walked the half-mile to the cemetery as the sky darkened and the wind picked up, slicing through everyone's clothes. We gathered around the grave and the coffin was lowered on ropes. At that moment it began to snow, large, whirling flakes which had covered the earth mound by the time Father Frank finished his eulogy. Everybody then filed past the open grave, tossing in a handful of earth onto the coffin as they walked by. The snow was coming down harder and harder. Everything was perfect, just as it should be for a funeral: cold, grey, snowy, and uncomfortable for the living.

After the burial, in keeping with tradition, there was a party at the Calderon house. People ate and drank, and told tales of Don Genaro Calderon, laughing, crying, celebrating his life.

Two days later there was a knock on my door. It was Maria Calderon.

"Genaro liked you, and I want you to have something that belonged to Genaro, something you can remember him by. You have been working on your house, so I bring you this." She handed me a beat up, twenty-five-foot tape measure with Genaro's name scratched on the side. "He had it for many years," she said. "There is much of his spirit in it."

I held it, unable to speak for a moment, barely able to see. "Thank you," I managed to croak.

"I want to thank you," she continued, "and to say goodbye."

"Goodbye?"

"My children say I can't live here by myself anymore. They are taking me to California."

"California!"

"I don't want to go. I don't belong in California; I belong here." Her voice was cracking. "I was born here, I was married here, my children were born here, my husband died here and is buried here. My whole life is here. I want to die here and be buried next to my husband."

"But Maria, you don't have go! We would watch over you and take care of you, all of us."

"I know you would, but you're not family, and my children don't believe they can count on you to do it." She held out her hand. "My children are waiting in the car to take me to California." She turned and started walking away, and then she stopped, turned, and said plaintively, "I don't want to die in California. I want to die here."

I watched her walk away stiffly in her black dress toward the car waiting to take her away far from her home. But her children were right—we were not her family, and even though at the moment we could pledge to watch over her and really mean it, we could also leave La Perla at any time and never return. We did not have the iron bond that family brings. We could not guarantee her family anything. Once Genaro died, there was no place for Maria, not even in La Perla, and certainly not in California.

Babe

Babe was nineteen and looked thirty-five. She came to La Perla for a Spring Equinox Party with someone she had met in Albuquerque the night before. She got so drunk at the party she passed out, and since no one knew her, no one took her home. She slept on Louie's floor uncovered with a thin blanket. Her overnight stay stretched into days and then into weeks.

She was from Sherman, Texas, and ran away from home at thirteen and went to Dallas where she became a go-go dancer/hooker. For five years she made her way around Texas and the South, dancing and screwing for shelter, food, and drinks, especially drinks. She came to Albuquerque as a groupie with ZZ Top, got drunk at the after-concert party, took off her clothes, jumped on a table and started dancing. She was doing a Rockette's kick when she fell off the table and injured her back. No more dancing, no more high kicks, no more ZZ Top.

After her mishap, she stayed in Albuquerque. She had not contacted her family in over five years and was too stubborn to contact them now. The only skills she had were sexual, so she relied on them and the kindness of strangers for shelter. While crashing at somebody's place she met a friend of Tommy's who knew about the Equinox Party. So she came to La Perla, another lost bit of humanity looking for a place.

There was no booze in La Perla, and the nearest liquor merchant was twelve miles away. There was little money among the freaks, and at the time, there were no running vehicles. The guy who sold the beer, Hyman Addio, was the quintessential dirty old man—married—who would have screwed her for a six-pack, but the road from La Perla to his store was little traveled and a terrible road to hitchhike on. Twelve miles each way is a long, long way to walk when you've got the shakes from alcohol withdrawal. So want to or not, Babe was forced to dry out.

It was not easy. She was sick for several days, shaking and puking, but gradually she started coming out into the sun. At first she came out to the garden where I was working and talked, but soon she was in the garden working with me. I provided her with an ear as she talked about getting her life together, starting over. She talked happily, carried along by her own voice. She talked of gardens and country living, and peace and harmony, and living a meaningful, spiritually fulfilling life. I listened noncommittally, giving an occasional grunt as we worked in the hot sun.

She made me nervous. Her face was ravaged and her voice whiskey-ground and graveled, but she still had the body of a nineteen-year-old. When she worked in the garden she wore a pair of cut-off jeans that just barely covered her ass. I would watch her bend over to pull a weed or squat down to plant a seed, and I would have to force my mind back to the task at hand. I had been several months without a woman, as a matter of choice. My life was now neat and ordered, and I wanted to keep it that way. I knew for certain that bringing a woman into it would destroy that order. Sexual relations always became messy and would send my life spinning off in some unpredictable, uncontrollable direction. I had broken off having sex with Jill in an attempt to take more control over my life. We remained friends. Touchy and uneasy, but still friends. But now sex was raising its seductive head in my garden.

Babe drifted from one household to another, eventually sleeping with all the single men in La Perla, except me. I was probably closer to her than anyone else in town, but sex between us was an unspoken no-no. It was as if we had made an agreement without ever discussing it. Only once did we ever even talk about sex. We were working in the garden when the subject came up.

"You've been here three weeks," I said. "All the single guys here are looking for a female partner. I'm surprised you've lasted this long without hooking up with one of them."

She reddened. "I guess I sleep around too much."

"That's not what I meant. I'm just surprised that you're not hooked up with someone, that's all."

"What about you? You're not hooked up either."

"I guess I just don't want the complications. My life is pretty simple now, and I want to keep it like that. Although I do get tempted." I glanced at her quickly.

"I've been thinking about sex," she said, growing a deeper red. "I think maybe I'll stop sleeping with different guys. I just don't know how to get by without using sex. But if a girl sleeps around, guys don't take her seriously. They just see a piece of ass." She stood up quickly. "I gotta go now."

I watched her walk away in her tiny cut-offs. We never talked about sex again.

She continued helping me in the garden, spinning out her dreams and plans for a new life. It was easy to see the change in her now. She had color in her face and was looking more and more like the nineteen-year-old she was, and less like the worn-out hooker she had been. I listened and said little.

Our relationship continued to play out in my garden in an awkward, uneasy fashion. I would sneak looks at her in those damned cut-offs, and the conflict between sexual desire and the desire for the simplicity that came from not having sexual relationships intensified. And strangely enough, she seemed to get more demure and shy the more we worked together. Whenever she caught me looking at her, or when I noticed her looking closely at me, she flushed and turned away. She had stopped sleeping with the single men and was staying with Ron and Cindy in their spare room.

One night there was a party at a commune in *Bosque*, about fifteen miles away. We all piled into several vehicles and made a caravan to the party. There was lots of music, grass, and booze. Both Babe and I got drunk. On the way back to La Perla she sat on my lap in the backseat, holding me and whispering over and over again, "You're a good man, you're a good man." By the time we got back to La Perla I was aching with the erection she had caused.

She stayed with me that night. I did not make love with her; I *screwed* her, part of me cool and uninvolved, and part of me driven by sexual pressure. There was no tenderness, no soft words, no gentle caresses. The sex seemed to go on for hours, but in spite of my sexual deprivation, I was not able to ejaculate. She tried everything she knew in her extensive bag of tricks, but nothing worked. I watched her struggling in the lamplight until the sweat was dripping off her onto me. Finally, I gave up, rolled over, and went to sleep.

I woke up late the next morning, badly hungover. I was alone in my bed. When I went outside I saw Babe leaning against the fence, looking at my garden. When she saw me walking toward her she burst out crying. I was flustered, not knowing why this was happening. She started talking rapidly, telling me that she was going to Albuquerque to get a job waitressing or something like that, something legit. She would save her money and buy a house in La Perla, and then I would see what kind of person she really was. I said nothing. She turned and walked away. That afternoon, she caught a ride out of town.

Six months later I got a letter from her, from Sherman, Texas. She was pregnant, didn't know who the father was, and had gone home in desperation to her parents' ranch in Sherman. It had been six years since her parents had seen or heard from her. She was leaving Sherman soon and was coming back to La Perla. She did not want her child born a bastard in Sherman. Her child was to be born in La Perla, only La Perla would do.

I never saw nor heard from her again.

Weeds

When I planted my garden in La Perla it was the first time I had ever grown anything other than a few flowers around whatever house I was renting. As an academic person in my previous life I had absolutely no interest in such pursuits. That was something bored housewives and ancient grandfathers did to occupy their time, but not something those of us who dwelt in the realms of the mind concerned ourselves with. But in La Perla, the connection between what you grow and what you eat was not only obvious, it was obviously necessary. The grocery store is not the source of food; it is merely the intermediary between the soil and your stomach—although modern supermarkets may be intermediary between a chemical lab and your stomach, the chemist as replacement for the farmer.

In La Perla I learned great respect and admiration for those who grow our food and for the whole, magical process of soil, seed, plant, food. A farmer is often a heavy equipment operator, a good shade tree mechanic, a welder, an astute weatherman, and a sharp businessman. Forget the image of the hayseed with a battered hat and a straw twig drooping out of his mouth, in his greasy overalls and manure-coated boots. Most of the farmers I know today are college educated. The farmer is to be extolled. Growing food is an ancient profession, even older than prostitution. And weeding is an adjunct to that profession, one that I learned in La Perla, and continue to practice forty years later.

I spend a lot of time in the summer weeding in my yard

and garden. I snip them with shears, I root them up and root them out, or, these days, I whack them with my gasoline-powered weed cutter. I absolutely refuse to spray poisonous chemicals on my property. That is too much like modern warfare, like spraying Agent Orange on one's own troops just to kill jungle. But within a week or two of my weed destruction and devastation, fresh, vigorous new weeds replace the ones I slaughtered. So back I go to the battlefields, attacking with my heavy duty, non-ergonomic weed whacker, or getting down on my knees for close, hand-to-hand combat, understanding fully that the enemy will re-group and return again no matter how many casualties I cause, thereby begging the question: Why do I do it if victory can never be achieved? Am I merely like Sisyphus pointlessly pushing my boulder up the hill?

The first answer to the question is the most obvious. If I don't do the weeding, the weeds will overrun my garden and I will not get as much produce. But on the other hand, the amount of work in growing a garden would be greatly reduced if I ignored the weeding. I do less work, but I get less food. In that statement lies a basic fact of life. The choices I make daily invariably involve trade-offs: I get this, but I give up that. And often the choice I should make, the best choice in the long haul, is the one that requires the most toil and sweat. So, at the simplest level, weeding my garden is a practical activity. I want my garden to be as productive as it can be. But there are other, more complex levels in my motivation for weeding.

There is aesthetics. I not only want my garden to be productive, I want it to look like a garden. Weeds are the antithesis of a garden. They are gross, rank, and unruly. They refuse to grow in neat, orderly rows. They spread over everything, masking and mocking the human effort to control just that little piece of earth. I need a clear demarcation between wild nature and ordered nature. I want to be able to stand back and see the neatness of order, the blessed rage for order that combines man-made beauty with the natural. I want to feel pride in I what I have labored to produce.

Weeding makes me feel that I am fighting against an attitude that is destructive of the human desire to live in a spirit of harmony and sharing. Weeds don't want to co-exist with other plants. They want to dominate, to overwhelm, to be the only plant growing in that plot of land. They invade their neighbors in seeking to build an empire where they and only they will rule. This does not imply that I too behave like weeds in wanting only my plants in the garden plot and no others. My weeding is defensive, not aggressive. If the weeds stay out of my garden, out of my yard really, I am quite willing to let them live their lives in peace. I do not leave the boundaries of my territory to try to take theirs.

Weeding teaches me some basic truths about life. I have noticed that where there is plenty of water, weeds grow thick and lush, but their roots are shallow, while the roots of water-stressed plants are deep and tough. It is easy to pull weeds up by the roots in well-watered areas, while pulling up the roots of water-stressed weeds is a much more difficult endeavor. These roots hold tight, and when I pull on them, the roots will snap a few inches underground, and the weed will return in a few days. To get at these roots, to eliminate the weed entirely, I need digging implements and hard work. These weeds are like Ezra Pound's "un-killable infants of the poor." They are truly into survival. In contrast, where life is easy, death is swift.

Weeding makes me think about how we define things. Pests are any creatures that annoy or bother us, that do not contribute to whatever goals we set, and in fact, have no interest in our goals. A rabbit in a stew pot is food; a rabbit in my garden is a pest. Weeds are any plants that grow where I don't want them to grow. By this definition, the species of elm that grows in central New Mexico is a weed. Elm seedlings appear everywhere, in countless numbers. If you don't pull them up when they are a few inches tall, they put down tree roots, and then you need to dig them up. Every year the elms begin the spring with new green, bright and lovely, but in a few weeks the leaves, under attack by elm beetles, become translucent like fine lace. It is a paradox tree. The mature tree is sick and unhealthy, but you cannot kill it. You can cut it down at ground level, but it always comes back. The quintessential weed. Cherry tomatoes are a wonderful fruit, but like weeds, they want to dominate other plants. When volunteer cherry tomato plants appear among my bell peppers, they become weeds. It is merely a matter of definition. Thus, weeding helps me see that if I want to change my attitude toward something, I must adjust how I define that thing.

Weeding helps me focus on aspects of life that I feel are fundamental and true. Weeding is not like Sisyphus pushing his stone up the hill. I will never, ever eliminate all weeds from my garden, but then I am not trying to. I understand that what we define as weeds may serve purposes that have nothing to do with my garden, purposes that are beyond my limited knowledge and understanding. I take comfort in seeing that the life force that informs the earth is so strong and ubiquitous that I, with my hands, my tools and machines, can only partially control the small portion of the world allotted to me, and that only with a great deal of effort. The effort is to control, not eradicate. It is all very existential. I weed as if my efforts had a meaningful, lasting effect, all the while knowing that the weeds will always come back. My little battles in the garden take on heavy symbolic meanings. I understand that if I don't do it constantly, the weeds will dominate. Metaphorically, so much of life seems to me to be devoted to that end: Don't let the weeds take over, even though that battle can never be won. As Candide exhorts us, we must cultivate our gardens, no matter what.

Weeding helps me see life as never-ending cycles, not as a straight line always moving upward. Progress is, after all, a man-made idea imposed on the world. Weeds and weeding are part of a cycle that the gardener moves on, and it will never end, nor should it. Being part of a *cycle* is not being in a *rut*. The seasons, the solar system, the galaxy, and I suspect, the universe itself, operate on natural cycles endlessly; a rut is an unnatural, man-made social condition. By seeing myself and my garden as parts of an endless cycle, I can toil in my garden and still exult in weeds' refusal to be extinguished.

Weeding helps me make essential distinctions, to differentiate among things in similar classes. Weeds are not just weeds. There are different kinds of weeds, and I find I react differently to the different types. Some weeds, like the goat-head thorn, I despise. Goat-heads are emblematic of the human impact on the environment. You never see goat-heads where human traffic is sparse. You can walk for miles in an isolated desert and never see one goat-head. However, they abound on commonly-used paths and roadways, where people pick them up on their shoes and clothing and tires and distribute them wherever they go. They are a natural and unnatural part of the natural world. Whenever I see a goat-head plant, I stop whatever I am doing and pull it up, making sure I get all of the root.

And there is a type of plant that I define as a weed, but which others may define as a flower, since it produces a pretty yellow bloom similar to a black-eyed Susan. But the flower has an unpleasant odor, and the plant has a highly developed root system that grows so deep the roots have to be dug out with a shovel, and so wide that roots may extend laterally for yards with new shoots springing up from them. If I don't make the effort to control it, it will quickly take over my entire yard. And since this, by definition, is what makes it a weed, I attack it with determination, no matter how much superficial beauty it may have.

Some weeds are breathtaking in their refusal to be obliterated. The silver nightshade is a plant I have a great deal of admiration and respect for. It has virtually no lateral roots, but its tap roots go down deep, very deep. I have never been able to get to the bottom of a nightshade root, not even digging with a shovel.

It has a breakaway root, i.e., before you can pull up the plant, the root breaks, and no matter how minuscule the piece of root left in the ground, it will come back. It has a lovely flower, a purple star-shaped bloom with a bright golden center, but it also has small, almost invisible bristles that grow like fine hair along the stem and on the leaves. If you grab the stem or touch the leaf, these bristles will pierce the skin and leave you with a painful itch. Like the rose, it is a combination of beauty and self-protection: Among roses be a rose, among thorns be a thorn.

However, if I don't try to control it, one plant will produce literally hundreds of offspring, each as difficult to remove as the parent. There are individual nightshade plants that I have been fighting for years. I cut them down before they can go to seed, which means cutting them a half dozen times a year, but the same plant always comes back in the same location. This weed is truly into survival, and I admire its beauty, its defenses, and its refusal to give up. One can, after all, admire and respect one's enemies.

In the central Rio Grande Valley of New Mexico, in the farm belt, the primary weed is the wild morning glory, or more commonly, bindweed. The perfect name for this weed. It creeps and crawls over everything, binding other weeds to it. This is another weed I admire as a truly worthy adversary. It seems so delicate, running low to the ground, with its small but plentiful blooms covering the ground with a carpet of violet and white flowers. But its delicate beauty is a ruse. Its root system is awesome, and it reproduces by spreading its seeds and by sending up shoots from its lateral roots which extend for distances that only God knows the measure of. It stays low to the ground until it comes across something vertical, which it will climb up and cover. I consider it our version of the kudzu of the Southeastern U.S., or the tangen-tangen of the South Pacific. This is my most ardent enemy, and yet my admiration for it is such that it borders on love.

Weeding is a labor of Sisyphus only if I foolishly believe that I can eradicate all those plants I define as weeds. Weeding is not an exercise in dominating nature; it is rather the attempt to assert a modicum of control over one tiny plot of earth I call my garden. It is a daily lesson I derive, and a meditation on the world, the physical world and the world of meanings and understanding. It helps me coexist in this world in peace and harmony, even with those I might define as enemies.

Bindweed and Me

Mornings I hunker in the rows
and go to battle,
sharp-edged tool in hand,
damned by my foreknowledge
that in the end comes failure.
I dig deep, I pull and tear,
but in the end
the bindweed is still there,
patiently waiting underground
should I relax my vigilance.
Somewhere in the wilderness
the Mother Weed is growing,
spreading roots throughout the world
until they reach our little gardens
and we go forth into the rows
to hold the bindweed back
to keep a semblance of control.

O Mother Weed
I make a pact with you:
Ease up on me and let my garden grow,
hold back your children,
teach them moderation
and I will once more let them be
the wild and lovely
Morning Glory.

Spence

He told us his name was Spencer, Spencer Duvall, and that he was from Mississippi. He first came to La Perla for a Thanksgiving Feast, which usually brought in anywhere from fifty to seventy-five people for the day from as far south as Socorro and as far north as Albuquerque. Spence had heard about the feast through the underground news service, commonly called the Hippie Grapevine, in Albuquerque and had come along with several folks for the party.

Like many of the social misfits who came to La Perla for the first time, he fell in love with the place. Here was a backwater apart from the social mainstream which flowed past it with no awareness of its existence. And like many of these misfits, he had a past that he thought he could escape from in La Perla. Spence certainly didn't look like someone hiding from his past. He was twenty years old and had sleepy eyes and dark blond hair with a forelock that kept drooping down over one eye. This gave him an air of youth and innocence, almost angelic. He looked like one of the kids from the *Our Gang* comedies grown up. He was soft-spoken, with a drawl that was pleasant to listen to and made him seem childlike and harmless. He did not return to Albuquerque immediately after the Feast but stayed at Ron and Cindy's place for several days, visiting people and just walking around town and the desert mesa. After a few days he got a ride back to Albuquerque. He returned two weeks later.

Ron and Cindy let him stay in the spare room in their home

while he began rebuilding and remodeling an ancient adobe hen-house and chicken coop behind their house. The adobe hen-house had slowly been melting back into the ground it originally came from until now there were only three walls standing in a U-shape covered by a leaky roof. Ron and Cindy had stretched chicken wire across the open end of the structure and used it as a chicken coop. Now the chickens were transferred to Tommy's coop across the road from Ron and Cindy's. After cleaning out the chicken shit, Spence began the job of rebuilding and remodeling the structure to make it his home. He worked hard on the building, mixing mud and making adobe bricks, repairing the ceiling, punching windows in the existing walls, and rebuilding the missing wall.

Spence was friendly and likable, but quiet and self-contained. Within a few days everyone in La Perla knew the outline of Spence's story. "Spencer Duvall" was an alias and he was wanted in Mississippi for some unspecified crime. He was running west, had made some friends in Albuquerque, and was now sure he had found the place to drop out of sight and make a new beginning—new home, new identity, new life. Whenever people gathered for dinner or to socialize and make music, Spence would be there, at the edge of the group, listening but rarely saying anything. He was accepted by everyone, no one ever questioned him about his past, and we figured it was only a matter of time before he felt himself a full member of the group.

All through the winter, when the weather permitted, he worked on his house, and slowly it began to take shape. By spring, he had repaired the roof, completed the fourth wall with a window and a door, and now had a weather-tight, enclosed space. The final stage was putting in the decking for a wooden floor. I would go visit him, sometimes helping and sometimes talking while he worked. He was always friendly, but remained generally solitary, and maintained a certain distance from everyone. As the spring equinox drew closer there was a corresponding rise in excitement in La Perla. Wintertime, the time of keeping still, the time of cabin fever, was coming to an end. The time of planting, rebirth, and growth was almost at hand. Everyone went around smiling as the winter shell began to break. Preparations for the Spring Equinox Party began a month before the equinox. Word-of-mouth invitations went out on the underground stream that flowed beneath the mainstream of Albuquerque and Socorro. Musicians were contacted, plans for food were laid out.

Like the Thanksgiving Feast, the Spring Party drew people from far and near. While Thanksgiving was more subdued, more of a family affair than the Equinox, the Spring Party was much wilder as people let out all the pent-up frustrations of winter. Music, there was always lots of music. There would be newly-formed and still-forming bands playing at different households throughout town. There was dancing, eating and pot smoking, and lots of loving going on all night. The party was a huge success.

One of the guests that year was a blonde belly dancer who called herself Francoise. She claimed to be from France and spoke with a funny French accent. She was draped in wispy strands of pastel rayon that revealed a set of hearty hips and breasts and a deep-bowled navel. Her blonde hair was long, halfway down to her waist, and she went about barefooted with little bells around her ankles that tinkled every time she moved.

That night Francoise did a number of swirling, feverish dances involving bells, drums, and finger cymbals. It was Spring and the sap was rising, especially for Spence. It was love at first sight. That night Francoise stayed with Spence.

Late the next morning I heard the tinkling sound of bells and cymbals coming down a dusty La Perla street. And there she was in all her shimmering pastel glory with Spence trotting behind, as happy as a puppy. She stayed for two days and then left to return to Dixon in northern New Mexico where she lived in a commune. Spence went with her.

Before he left Spence came to see Louie and me. He was leaving for a few days, he said, a couple of weeks maybe, but then he would return to complete his house. He shook hands, and he and Francoise drove off. Louie turned to me.

"Think we'll ever see him again?"

"Nope."

"Yeah. Me neither."

About a month later word trickled down to us that Spence was back in Mississippi. The commune in Dixon had been raided by police and drug agents. They found some fledgling marijuana plants and hauled everyone off to jail. They quickly found out that Spence was wanted on a drug charge. He had been serving time in Parchman Prison for selling marijuana, and he had escaped. He was extradited to Mississippi where the escape charge was added to the current sentence. He had five years to serve, with a possibility for parole after thirteen months.

One day I got a letter from Spence in prison, and we began a correspondence. His real name was Virgil, Virgil Kincaid, but I could think of him only as Spence. I sent him books: Krishnamurti, Zen, Sufism, poetry, and mythology. He wrote back poems, scenes of prison life, and general speculations on the Spirit. He wrote about how La Perla was still his dream, about his plans to return. He would keep his nose out of trouble, stay clean, and parole would be no problem. Once he wrote from the prison hospital. Some Black inmates had cornered him in the yard and beaten him severely because he refused to give up a nonexistent stash of cigarettes which they were sure he was hoarding. His main worry was that the incident might harm his chances for parole.

As the end of his thirteenth-month period approached, Spence's letters got more and more excited. He was positive he would be paroled. Soon he would be back in La Perla legally, and he would start working on his little house again. He would arrange to leave Mississippi as soon as he walked out of Parchman.

The thirteenth month came and went with no word from

Spence. Two more months passed. Then I got a brief letter, postmarked Parchman Prison. Spence had been paroled and stayed in Mississippi trying to get some money to come back to La Perla. Of course the first means of making money that he thought of was dealing dope, since that was what he had experience in, even though his experience with it had resulted in his incarceration. Of course he got busted again. Now he was considered a habitual criminal and was sentenced to twelve years without parole.

It was the last I ever heard of, or from, him. Spence was such a sweet young man that it was difficult for me to imagine what Parchman would turn him into. I wrote him several letters but quit writing after I got no response. And as the final, definite end to Spence's dream of La Perla, Ron and Cindy moved their chickens back to the stable, where they now had the ritziest coop and hen house in town.

La Perla Spring

Every spring the winds arrived with a force that always caught us off guard. They would start in late February and blow off and on all through March and April. On the days that it blew, which was most days, the wind usually started at about ten in the morning, beginning with a gentle breeze, then picking up force throughout the morning and late afternoon, then easing up gradually until around sunset when it subsided. In the evening everything would usually be hushed and peaceful, and sitting on the slope of the East Mesa I could hear voices floating up from clear across town and the tinkling of the bells on the ram as the sheep dog herded the sheep back to their pens for the night.

The next morning the winds would return, rolling in out of the southwest, driving a cloud of sand that stung so bad you had to keep your back to it. Your clothes billowed out like sails, dust filled the porches of your ears, grit ground between your teeth, under your gums, and in a few minutes the buffeting would leave you dazed and stupid. For the most part we sat out the wind indoors, but we still had the dust to contend with—it didn't sting and you couldn't see it in the air, but it settled on everything, coating the entire interior of the house with a fine, light powder. Dishes and utensils had to be rinsed before using, chairs had to be wiped before sitting. People spent a lot of time just staring out the windows.

Sometimes the wind would not blow for several consecutive

days, and what a blessing that was; other times it would blow for three days nonstop, day and night, a continuous roar that we went to sleep to and awoke to as the sand beat on the door and windows, while the dust sifted in through the tiniest cracks and openings, silent as death. I would read *Dune* for the third or fourth time, staring out at the opaque sand, hoping for something to happen, anything that would relieve the cabin fever. It was rumored that José Ignacio, who ran the local post office, would go completely berserk during one of these blows and try to outdo the wind in howling. It was said that his family had to lock him up in a room until the wind died. His reaction to the winds was a bit extreme, but we all understood it.

On the west side of the Rio Grande the sand had already completely covered up old Highway 85. If you drove south on it, the road ran into a sand dune and just disappeared. All around was nothing but sand. It was like an eerie scene from a post-apocalyptic science fiction movie or Shelley's "Ozymandias." The migration of the sand to the east was slowed by the Rio Grande, but there were now dunes on the east side of the river, about two miles south of La Perla, and they were moving toward town. We knew that in a short time—in geological, extra-human terms—La Perla too would be covered in sand and disappear, like old Highway 85. Ron's dead Volkswagen Beetle, parked behind his house for three years, had sand drifted up so high around it he could no longer open the doors without first digging it out. Eventually our houses would be covered over too. We could come and live here, make our homes here, but soon enough all traces of our having been here would be obliterated. This knowledge gave me the same pleasure that I got from seeing the deserted adobe houses in town slowly fall apart and melt back into the earth. It made me feel transient, but somehow a part of something eternal at the same time.

The winds taught us hard lessons in patience and acceptance. Nature determined what you did and when you did it. If you had anything to do outside, you did it before ten a.m. when the winds usually began. Once they started, there was nothing for it but to sit and wait it out. The spring winds also served as a filter, sifting out those who came and fell in love with La Perla's superficial rural peace, and its beauty. A two or three week encounter with wind, sand, dust, and cabin fever was usually enough to send them scurrying back to the comforts of Albuquerque. Only the hard core remained.

One day, in the middle of spring, a flashy new Buick drove into town. Like most people that came to La Perla, the driver, Bob, had gotten off the Interstate, gotten on a lonely state road and followed it until it dead-ended in the middle of town. The wind was not blowing that day, so Bob quickly became enchanted with La Perla. He hung out all day, walking around town, visiting the different households, talking about peace, harmony, and country living. He spent the night in Ron's house.

Bob was a refugee from civilization. He was from Detroit and had been working on an assembly line for several years making toll booths for turnpikes and bridges. He had been married for two years. One day when he got off work, instead of driving home to his wife, he found himself getting on an Interstate heading west. He had no conscious plan and no particular destination. The thought of toll booths, Detroit, house payments, wife, and responsibilities became more than he could handle. So he did what millions of his American forebears had done: He went west.

The morning after his arrival, while the air was still and clear and fresh, he decided he wanted to take an overnight hike to Ladron Peak, rising starkly out of the desert floor some twenty miles away. *El Ladron*, the thief, was the mountain that provided hiding places for the robbers who held up the Socorro stagecoach one hundred years earlier. We suggested that an overnight hike was not a good idea this time of year.

"Hey man," said Louie, "Ladron is really isolated. There's

nothing out there but rattlesnakes and buzzards. It's spring and it really gets windy this time of year. And the mountain looks close, but it's twenty miles away. It is not a good idea to be walking around in the desert in spring."

But the morning was so calm and still, and in the clear air Ladron seemed just a stroll away, and Bob would have nothing to do with sound advice. No one in La Perla pressed him on the matter. Everyone had the right to do what he wanted, even if it was stupid. As Joel used to put it, "This is America. Everyone has the right to build his own prison." So if this half-assed Easterner (we thought of anyone living east of New Mexico as "Easterners") wanted to go on a hike, well, that was his business.

Bob borrowed Ron's camping gear and took off hiking southwest toward Ladron. The wind started up about two hours after he left. It began gently and built up gradually. By noon it was howling, and the blowing sand was like a solid wall. It blew all night without let-up.

The next morning I stumbled against the wind across town to Ron's house. It was slow going with my eyes three-quarters shut in a futile attempt to keep the sand out. Bob had not returned. He did not return all that day, and the wind continued to blow all day and all the following night. And again, the following morning I staggered to Ron's house. Bob had still not returned.

The wind blew all day again, and by afternoon we were all worried, but no one had any interest in going to Ladron to look for him. We could get lost just as easily as he in the wind, and besides, his predicament was of his own devising.

Once more the sun went down, and once more the wind didn't, until finally, around ten that night, the wind stopped and everything was eerily quiet. I fell asleep to be awakened well after midnight by a car driving into town. A few minutes later I heard it drive up the mesa and out. I drifted back to sleep, to be awakened shortly before sunrise by another car driving out of town. I went back to sleep.

It was late morning before I was up and on my way to Ron's house. I noticed that Bob's car was gone. When Ron saw me he chuckled, which was about as wild an expression of merriment as Ron ever exhibited.

"He came in about one this morning, crashed on the floor with all his clothes on, and left about sunrise. He gobbled some eggs, gave me some money to pay for losing all my camping gear, jumped in his car and split. I think La Perla had lost its charm."

"He lost all of your gear?"

Another chuckle. "Yeah. He had quite a time."

Bob was about halfway to Ladron when the wind started. It was not very strong at first, so he kept on going, and by the time he got to the mountain, the wind was blowing hard, very hard. He took shelter against some rocks out of the wind, but when he saw that the wind was only getting stronger, he decided to climb a ways up Ladron to see if he could get above the blowing sand and get his bearings. He left all the camping gear behind except his canteen of water.

"I'm surprised he had enough sense to keep that with him," said Ron.

No matter how high Bob climbed he was still hammered by the sand and wind. When he came back down, he could not, of course, find the camping gear. The sleeping bag, the pack with all his food, matches, everything was lost somewhere at the foot of Ladron. He spent that night, the next day, the next night and the day following carefully rationing his water and looking for shelter from the wind at night, and for his gear and the route back to La Perla by day. He failed on all counts. After the wind stopped that night, he managed to get to Interstate 25 where, dazed and half-coherent, he flagged down a car and paid the driver twenty dollars to drive him to La Perla, about ten miles away.

Ron told me Bob's tale with a sardonic grin. "He said he was going back to Detroit. I think toll booths and a wife didn't sound so bad after all. I guess freedom was not as much fun as he imagined. Hey, no wife, no job, no responsibilities. Just go out for a stroll on a sunny spring day—what could be better?"

On my way back home I was thinking about the *Bible*. Ecclesiastes tells us that there is a time and a season for every purpose under heaven. Whatever you do you should do it in the right season of your life, whether it's quitting your job, leaving your wife, or taking a stroll in the wilderness. It sounds like good, sound advice to me. Wonder why it's so hard for people to accept that?

Ladron at sunset Photo courtesy of Bob Christensen

The Eyes of Jesus

Eva Perea, in her early forties, was the youngest single woman from the original families of the slowly expiring town. José Garcia, also in his forties, was the youngest single man. Their families had roots in La Perla which went back some two hundred years. Naturally they gravitated toward each other. Eva and José had been "secret" lovers for about four years. Eva was actually married, but her husband had run off with a woman from Albuquerque ten years earlier. Since Eva was a devout Catholic she had never filed for divorce and still considered herself a married woman even though she had no inkling of her husband's whereabouts. José had been a widower for about six years.

In keeping with the conservative morality of the community, their love affair could not be open and free, but was conducted "in secret": At night, José would sneak from his house to Eva's, creep in the back door, and spend the night with his lady love. In the morning he would arise before dawn and sneak back to his own house. When he left his house in the morning, he would make a loud production out of leaving through the front door of his home so the townspeople would know he had spent the night, chastely, in his own home and bed.

Of course, everyone in town knew what was going on, and every evening the town folk would peer through the raised slats of their Venetian blinds as José did his lover's pilgrimage down the back paths, across now vacant lots with their adobe ruins, Gothic in the moonlight, to Eva's.

This ritual had been going on for four years, but no one ever talked about it. It seemed so natural now that it no longer inspired any gossip. If there were a social event of any sort, people always made sure to invite both of them. Eva and José would go to friends' homes for dinner, separately, socialize and be friendly with each other, but give no hint of the true nature of their relationship. After dinner, they each would go to their separate houses, and then José would do his secret journey to Eva's.

Eva was a truly religious woman, and eventually this illicit love began to weigh heavier and heavier on her soul. For a while she had managed to push back her fears and guilt, but now they were resurfacing. Naturally gregarious and cheerful, she was becoming increasingly quiet and morose. She stopped accepting invitations to parties and dinners. There were dark circles around her eyes and she was looking haggard. She no longer went to the post office at ten in the morning to get her mail. Since there was no mail delivery in the town, going to the post office (which was about the size of a roomy bathroom) and picking up the mail at ten was a daily ritual that brought the people together for a morning chat and gossip.

Eventually Eva felt forced to ask José to stop coming over for a while. "I have to deal with the sin of what we are doing." The terrible part of all this for Eva was that she had to endure her torments alone. There was no one in town to confide in. We all knew what was going on, but we couldn't tell her that. Her shame would be unbearable. She had confessed her sin to the priest, but he had merely mumbled something about being strong against the temptations of the flesh and the seductiveness of Satan and told her to say she forgot how many "Hail Marys" and "Our Fathers." The experience had not left her feeling cleansed.

The townspeople sympathized with her moral struggles, and we suffered with her in silence, and we prayed for her, each in our own fashion. Unknown to her, her moral dilemma had become the town's dilemma. Everyone could see that she and José were destined to be lovers, even if somewhat star-crossed. The aging community *needed* them to be lovers.

Every morning at six Eva would walk to the empty church and kneel before the crucifix, praying with all her strength for guidance. *What,* she would plead, *should I do O Lord? How can love be such a sin? It's not just the flesh O Lord. I love José, I want to spend my life with him, but Your Church tells me I cannot divorce my husband who abandoned me and go to a new husband. How can something which feels so right be so wrong? Help me O Lord, tell me what to do, give me a sign, anything, I beg You.*

José, meanwhile, walked around distracted and confused. He tried to be his usual happy self, but with little success. His problem was not religious—he had no qualms whatsoever about his love for Eva or over their sleeping together; his only concern was for Eva's emotional, physical, and spiritual well-being. He felt guilty because in making love with Eva he had pushed her to a spiritual crisis. And now he was scared that he was losing the love of his life.

So everyone watched and waited. Perhaps Eva's prayers would be answered, perhaps Jesus would show her the way, but to the people in the town it seemed that it would take a miracle for this to happen.

And then the miracle happened.

One morning Eva went to the storage shed behind her house to look for some misplaced utensil. As she approached the shed she looked up and stopped cold in her tracks. She stood frozen for a moment, then dropped to her knees, crossed herself, and began praying with tears running down her cheeks. There, in the cracking, peeling paint of the door to the shed, was the clear and unmistakable image of the face of Jesus.

He was looking down at her, but instead of the love and pity she had dreamed she would see in his eyes, his gaze was stern, accusing. She knelt there for a long time, praying as hard as she could, the words coming out in rush, almost unintelligible, as she told Jesus what she and José had been doing, and how their sin had burdened her, and how she needed strength and guidance. *What should I do Lord? What should I do?*

She stood up and walked to the door, gazing into Jesus' eyes. She turned, and with tears streaming, went looking for José. At that moment she didn't care if the townspeople saw her pulling him to her house by his arm. José stood in front of the shed astonished at the clarity of the image. He walked up to the door and looked intently into Jesus' eyes. They were cold and unrelenting.

"It's the sign I've been waiting for!" she whispered fiercely. "But what does it mean? What is he telling me?" She turned to José and broke into sobs. "I think He's telling me that I can't be with you anymore."

"No, no!" said José. "That can't be! How can Jesus be against love?"

"But what we're doing is wrong! It's a sin! José, I'm a married woman."

"Married! That *cabron* deserted you years ago. If you're married to anybody it's to me. How can my love for you be wrong? Doesn't love purify everything? Isn't Jesus the Prince of Love?"

Eva started crying again. "But his eyes, José, look at his eyes! In the eyes of the Church I'm a married woman! I don't know what to do, but I cannot go against Mother Church!" She turned and ran into her house.

José stood staring glumly at the eyes of Jesus. The eyes of Jesus stared back, unmoved, into the eyes of José.

In a few days everyone in the *Rio Abajo*, the river valley south of Albuquerque, knew about the face of Jesus, and Eva's back yard became a place of pilgrimage. People came from as far south as Polvadera and Escondido, and as far north as Veguita and Las Nutrias to stand and kneel before the image. They wanted to see

Eva, she who had been so honored by this visitation, but Eva remained locked in her house, refusing to respond to the entreaties of the pilgrims.

Two weeks passed, and for Eva the daily visitors were a torment. She wished only to be alone, to pray for forgiveness, to do whatever penance the spirit told her to do. The townspeople rarely saw her, and then only in quick glimpses. And poor José was an emotional wreck. The community suffered along with them, confused that what should have been an occasion for great celebration—the appearance of the Savior—had brought nothing but malaise to the town. Everyone suffered from lovesickness.

The excitement over the image was gradually dying away and fewer and fewer pilgrims came to pay their respects. And the image itself was slowly fading. Then one day, two weeks after the Lord's appearance, Eva looked out her kitchen window over the heads of a small cluster of pilgrims at the image and her eyes widened. Something was different about the image. She looked more closely, squinting her eyes. Yes. The image had changed, the eyes had changed.

She waited until the worshipers had left, and then went to the shed door and looked at His eyes. They were softer now, and the whole face seemed suffused with sympathy. She knelt down, gazing up at the face. Then the rain that had been threatening all day began to fall, a gentle drizzle that cooled the warm, humid air. As she watched, the eyes of Jesus welled with tears that ran slowly down His cracked wooden cheeks. Jesus was weeping for her! He understood!

She ran to José's house, and once again pulled him by the arm to her back yard. By now the rain was coming down hard, plastering her hair to her face. "Look!" she shouted at a startled José, "Look!"

José looked up at the image. The eyes had grown larger, and the tears had a reddish tint, like blood. Eva stood next to José and timidly reached up and gently touched the face of Jesus. She looked in His eyes, and this time it was not a stern accusation she saw, but a wave of love that washed over her. José was right, there was no anger or disappointment in those eyes, only love. And suddenly she knew.

"You're right, José, you're right! He's telling us love is good, our love is good. She fell to her knees. *"O querido Jesus! Gracias, gracias, gracias!"*

José pulled her to her feet and they stood in a wet, wild, laughing embrace.

So once again José made his nightly love pilgrimage to Eva's. Once again Eva was cheerful and charming, once again José went about town smiling, and once again the town settled happily into its quiet, lingering life.

Eventually the sun and rain obliterated the image until all that remained were two circles that had been the luminous and loving eyes, keeping watch over Eva and her home.

Showers

One of the hassles of living in old adobe houses in La Perla was that they were built before indoor plumbing was common in private homes. Many of the houses had added plumbing for the kitchen, but the outhouse was still common to most households. Of course, this meant no bathtub or shower. In summer, most bathing was done in outdoor, solarheated showers, and in winter one bathed in a tin tub in the kitchen.

Most of the houses in La Perla had neither natural gas nor propane tanks. The heating and cooking was done with wood stoves. Whenever a stove was lit, either a heating stove or kitchen stove, one of the first things you did was put a pot of water on it. You never knew when you would need or want hot water, so you developed a "hot water consciousness."

In winter a stove was always burning in one room, while the doors to other rooms were closed to conserve heat and firewood. Everyone would congregate in the heated room, usually the kitchen. Since the wood stove was lit, and it was foolish to waste heat, there was almost always something cooking or baking. Whenever I stepped into a kitchen from the freezing weather outdoors, my glasses would instantly fog up, and the smell of cooking beans or corn bread or a pan of brownies baking would be the prelude to an invitation to stay and eat a bit. And always there was the huge pot of hot water for coffee, washing dishes, or bathing.

In summer, of course, one used the cook stove as little as possible, and cooking was generally done before sunrise or after sunset when the air was cool. But in summer, as in winter, the pot of water was on the stove. An outdoor shower in summer might be as simple as a black hose coiled on the roof of a crude shower stall, a sort of stockade made of *latillas*, thin, straight tree branches erected for privacy. The hose, or a small tank, would be filled with water, and the heat of the sun would warm it up during the day, and in the evening you could take a warm, but short, shower. Gravity would run the water down through the shower head in a weak trickle.

After a while in La Perla, you would start dreaming of showers in which you had all the steaming hot water you wanted, merely by turning on a tap. Every time I visited friends in the city, the first thing I would do is take a long, leisurely shower. La Perla did that to you; you learned to appreciate the wonderful luxury of things most people rarely thought about.

Sometimes the search for a good shower could turn into an adventure. One hot summer day I was working in my garden when Frank stopped by in his truck wanting to know if I needed anything from Socorro since he was going into town. Cindy was sitting in the cab beside him. When I said no, there was nothing I needed, Cindy spoke up.

"How about a good shower? Wouldn't you like a long, hot shower? That's why I'm going to town. You want to come along?"

"Where are you planning to take a shower?"

"Oh, I know a place. They won't mind if you take one too."

I assumed she was going to a friend's house. "Boy! That does sound good. Let me get a towel and a change of clothes."

When we got to Socorro, Cindy asked Frank to drop us off at the School of Mines. She led me to a men's dorm and walked in the door without hesitation. We walked down a hallway with rooms on either side. As we walked past one room with an open door, there were three students talking.

Cindy waved. "Hi guys."

They stared gaping. To say that Cindy was voluptuous would be a horrid understatement. They mumbled some startled replies.

I looked back at the door thinking that we sure as hell did not look like students at New Mexico Tech. My hair was long and unkempt, my clothes ratty and torn, and Cindy's bra-less breasts, granny skirt, and combat boots did not give her the appearance of a co-ed. Cindy seemed totally unconcerned however. She turned into a doorway and I went in after her. We were in the first-floor dorm bathroom. There was a row of six sinks, a series of toilet stalls, and another row of small shower stalls, each with a curtain.

Cindy grinned at me and started taking off her clothes.

"Wait a minute! What about those guys in the room? They might report us to the dorm cops, or something."

"Naw. They're just college students. They don't know shit. Come on, take your clothes off."

Cindy was naked before I had removed my shoes. She let down her red hair, and with large, heavy breasts swaying she walked into one of the shower stalls and drew the curtain. I heard the water come on. I disrobed, wondering how many different crimes I was going to be charged with for this little escapade.

As I walked past her stall, Cindy called out, "Hey. Would you wash my back?"

The stall was tight for two people, so we were kind of pressed against each other. She had just soaped up her breasts and they were glistening and slippery as they slid along my lower chest. I had known Cindy for two years, had gone skinny dipping with her a number of times, but never had I responded sexually to her. She was cute, friendly, and as I said, *voluptuous*. But she was Ron's lady. I realized that this reticence was mine, not hers, but I had abided by it. Now, to my surprise, I had an erection.

"Hey," she said, "looky here. And I thought I didn't turn you on." She handed me the soap. "Come on, wash my back. She turned her back to me, rubbing her breasts against me in the process.

I was assiduously soaping her back, being careful not to wash below her waistline and not to touch her with my erect penis. She pushed back and leaned forward, her hands on the wall, her rear pressed against me. I put the soap down.

Afterwards, we dressed and walked back down the hall. The three guys were now standing in the hallway, watching us walk out of the bathroom toward them. Cindy's long hair was still dripping, her rounded breasts had dampened the front of her blouse and were swaying as we walked past them. I walked beside her, ginning like a Cheshire cat.

She smiled at them and waved. "Bye guys."

They were too dumbfounded to respond, and just watched wide-eyed as we stepped out the door. Outside in the sunshine, Cindy spread her arms in the air above her, and threw back her head.

"God, I love a good shower!"

In Praise of Eve

After all my efforts to begin
to see beyond the sexual woman and her naked skin,
and after all attempts to understand her with my mind
(since she is the other half of humankind)
I remained distracted by externals
(or so I thought)
and wandered from the heart of that which matters….

Is sex no more than reflex of the nervous coil
and love the bestial deified,
the sexual lifted up to the sublime?
The sensual stretches out beyond the bounds of good
or common sense and understanding
shrivels in the rind. The mind is blown about
peripheries of reason's hell; Pavlov rings his bell,
the dogs begin to drool like actors set on cue.
I too, though primate of the higher kind,
will salivate to mental bells that clang
despite of differences or time or rage of mind.

So how should I begin to understand?
Begin at the beginning and see what lies at hand.

The Garden opens and the scene repeats;
the woman offers and the man does eat.
The wild chaotic father, erect and prostrate both at once,
will lie with mild, erotic mother
to finish trembling and undone…

Is this the fatal fall from innocence?
"Innocence" says laughing Eve with moist red mouth

and knowing wink (and O the flow of breast and haunch!)
"Innocence is but the doorway to experience."
"She rubbed me wrong," says sullen Adam to a somber God
chewing on his beard in righteous wrath
and slamming shut the door to paradise.

And in the fallen Garden flowers succumb in colors
to the blandishments of bees
and butterflies lie shivering in the sun
while straining wings beat passion on the ground.
The cock will tread the hen, the ram in rut will tup the ewe,
the mare will take the stallion
while Eve stirs the cosmic brew.

O the naked woman in her naked skin!

Soft and firm at once
Light and undulations
Rolling contours

The taste, feel, smell of skin

Skimming over skin
Swirling moist over skin
Dipping into skin
The nips and tucks of skin

Deep, hidden, lidded places of the skin

Skin that's loose and flaccid
Skin that tenses, puckers, bumps and grows erect
Skin that's young and supple and untried
Skin that's older, folded, thin along the bone
Skin that sags, dimples, grins, and wimples

Salt skin
Spice and pepper skin
Wet, dripping, nippled skin…
Heaven is a woman, infinite supine,
on whose naked skin I wander
small, delirious, mad in all fulfilled desires
rolling down her gentle slopes
tumbling over roundy rim of omphalos
rubbing up against her body hair
swimming, floating in the overflowing cup of love!

Love must have his origin
in the physics of the skin,
the outside fusing with the in,
the crux of sex, the cross and crossing over,
the melting of the two into the one.

So naked praise to naked mother Eve!

> Mother of mystery
> Loom of time
> Portal of love
> Bed of fruition
> Womb of life
> Giver and taker
> Renewer and redeemer

The power that lies between her thighs
fulfills the earth, keeps time and life
on their spinning, lurching course:
Lust provides the motive force
that leads the universe to birth.

Shane Revisited

Louie and I were returning from a trip to Socorro for groceries in his beat-up Rover when about two miles outside of La Perla we saw someone walking along the roadside. That a stranger should be walking along that isolated stretch of road was unusual enough, but this particular stranger would have been unusual anywhere. He had a white gauze bandage wrapped around his head from his eyebrows up. Another bandage with an opening for his mouth covered his face from below his nose to his chin. Only his nose, ears, and eyes were exposed. Another bandage was wrapped around his left hand.

"We're warped into a movie. It's *The Return of the Mummy*," I said as Louie came to a stop.

"Hi. Where ya headed?"

"Is this the way to La Perla?"

"Yeah. We live in La Perla. You want a ride?"

We took him into town while Louie questioned him openly. For Louie, all the area for miles around was his "back yard," and he had a right to know what any newcomer was doing there. He told us why he was in La Perla, but never mentioned the bandages.

His name was Michael, and he was looking for Ron and Cindy whom he had met about a week earlier in Albuquerque. They had invited him to come and stay for a while in La Perla. Ron and Cindy were not home, so I invited him to stay at my place until they returned. We sat outside on the back seat of a car which leaned against the south wall of my house and we talked. I had already grown used to his mummy look.

Michael was tall, lanky, bow-legged, and hard-muscled. He was built like what in fact he was—a cowboy from Casper, Wyoming, a very wild cowboy. He was the only person I ever knew who was actually "run out of town" by the local sheriff, just like in a western movie. The police drove him to the outskirts of Casper and told him that if they ever saw him in town again, they would come up with a reason to arrest him and throw him in jail.

He drifted into New Mexico where he took a job as a "mule," delivering illegal shipments of drugs across the border at Juarez to destinations in the U.S. He was driving a shipment of marijuana on the interstate from El Paso to Denver, had just driven through Albuquerque and was coming into the town of Bernalillo, about fifteen miles north of Albuquerque, when he looked in his rear-view mirror and saw several cars with flashing lights weaving through the traffic behind him—police cars in a big hurry.

Michael did not hesitate. He pulled onto the shoulder of the highway, jumped out of his vehicle, and took off running west, across an alfalfa field toward Bernalillo. He was about halfway across the field when he heard shots behind him. When he looked back, he saw several cops with guns, one leaning on the hood of his car, taking careful aim. He heard several slugs go buzzing past, and then felt a blow to his left hand. He ran some more, and when he looked back again, he saw several cops running after him. His hand was bleeding.

He made it across the field and into a residential neighborhood. Running down a sidewalk he saw a car pulling out of a driveway. He opened the passenger door and jumped in. The driver was a kid, sixteen, seventeen years old.

"The cops are after me man!"

The kid never said a word. He took one wide-eyed look at Michael and his bleeding hand, and stepped on the gas. The car peeled out in a scream of rubber. Michael looked back and saw a cop running around the corner at the end of the block, and then he and the kid were gone.

Michael tied a handkerchief tightly around his hand to staunch the bleeding, noting with relief that the bullet had only grazed a fleshy part of his hand and had broken no bones. They drove around Bernalillo for a while, trying to figure out what to do next. Finally, the kid had an idea. On the other side of the interstate, in the foothills of the Sandia Mountains maybe ten miles to the east, there was a hippie commune outside the village of Placitas. The kid's logic was simple: Hippies and cops don't get along, Michael had been shot by a cop, so therefore the hippies would be willing to help him. He drove Michael to the commune.

When they got to the commune, Michael stayed in the car while the kid went and knocked on the door of a house. Michael saw him talking to someone in the doorway, gesturing toward him, and then he and several people came hurriedly to the car. They looked very worried as Michael watched them approach. In a minute he understood why.

The leader of the commune, a man calling himself Ulysses S. Grant, had gone berserk that morning and killed two men with a high-powered rifle, and then fled into the hills. Cops were everywhere, in and out of the commune, combing the hills in the area. There was no way Michael could stay there. One of the men gave Michael directions to a cave in the hills, not on commune property, along with some food and water. This was the most they could do; Michael was on his own.

Michael thanked the kid (never did know his name) who drove back to Bernalillo and whatever hassles the cops might have for him there. Michael took the water, some sandwiches and fruit, and followed a hastily drawn map to the cave.

As Michael told his tale with no particular intensity and emotion, I began to understand why he was run out of Casper. He was truly a wild man—not evil or bad, just wild. He was articulate and intelligent, and to him, this was just another event in an eventful life. Life was, after all, meant to be eventful. That was its excitement and joy. Otherwise, why bother? Not an attitude conducive to easy living in any structured society.

By the time he got to the cave it was late afternoon, and Michael was so exhausted he was dizzy. He ate the sandwiches and fell asleep. He was awakened hours later, at night, by someone stumbling around in the pitch-black darkness of the cave. Still half-asleep he called out in the darkness.

"Who's there?"

The response was a stream of swearing, followed by a threat. "I'm gonna blow your fucking head off!"

Then began a bizarre, dangerous game of hide-and-seek. Michael, the hider, would lie still behind a rock in the cave while the seeker crashed around raving incoherently. It was the seeker's madness that probably saved Michael's life, since he didn't search as much as he raved. Michael could see the lighter darkness outside through the mouth of the cave, and when the opportunity arose, he made a dash for the cave entrance.

He ran out of the cave, fell and rolled a bit down the hillside, bruising his ribs and banging his head. He could still hear the madman raging, now outside the cave, so he got up and ran some more, tripping over rocks and cacti. The game of hide-and-seek continued for what seemed like hours, until the assailant finally left. Too tired to move, Michael fell asleep again, where he lay.

He awoke to someone kicking his bruised ribs. It was daylight, and the first thing he saw was a pair of shiny, round-toed boots a few inches from his face. His eyes ran up the boots, up a pair of black-clad legs, to the cap and grinning face of a state trooper pointing a gun at him. Michael was beginning to get very tired of people pointing guns at him.

"I got the son of a bitch!" the cop yelled. "Don't move Grant, or I'll blow your fucking head off!"

Two other state troopers materialized, and Michael began

trying to explain that he was not Ulysses Grant, but they ordered him to shut up. His hands were manacled, and he was pushed in a stumbling walk down the hill to a police car. They radioed in that they had apprehended the suspect and were bringing him in. Not until after they arrived at the temporary search headquarters did they realize he was not Grant. But they did find out that he was wanted for transporting dope, and that he had eluded the police the day before.

Michael was sentenced to three to five years in prison at Santa Fe, a notorious joint called "the Wall" by inmates. He served eighteen months and was paroled. It was because he was on parole that he wound up outside La Perla with a bandaged face.

He had to report once a week to his parole officer or get sent back to the joint. He was not permitted to leave the state without the knowledge or consent of his parole officer. But Michael was not a man who accepted restrictions or controls very well. His forebears were mythologized in songs, John Wayne movies, and legends, but in the 1970's, the individuality and need for freedom of the cowboy were nothing more than a threat to the harmony and cohesiveness of society. Wyoming didn't want him, and now New Mexico had to deal with him. The requirements of his parole were galling, but he was determined not to return to prison, where the restrictions were nightmarish. So he did his best to comply, but fell a tad shy of compliance.

He could not resist the temptation thrown in his path by a friend going to California for a weekend. Would Michael like to come along? You bet Michael would, as long as they were back before Tuesday when he had to report to his parole officer. No problem, they would be back by Monday.

After a wild weekend on the beaches of Southern California, they were heading back to New Mexico when they collided with another vehicle. Michael was unconscious for a few minutes, and when he came to he was lying on the pavement with blood streaming from his battered face. There were several people huddled around him, and when he focused his eyes he saw they were "hippies."

"Are you all right man?" asked a girl with long blonde hair falling straight down over her shoulders. She was kneeling beside him, holding his hand.

"Yeah, I guess I'm all right. I don't think I've got any broken bones."

"Hey, the cops are coming. Are you holding anything? Anything you want to get rid of?"

The siren from the police car was deafening. For a moment Michael thought the cop was going to run over him lying in the road. "My wallet," he said, "don't let the cops get my wallet." He was thinking of his parole officer. If the cops knew his name, they would run a check on him and find that he was on parole in New Mexico, and they would notify his parole officer and Michael would be back in the joint in Santa Fe.

The girl reached into his pocket and pulled out his wallet. As the cop walked up to them, she slipped the wallet beneath her long skirt which was puddled around her on the pavement. She stayed kneeling by him while the cop told him that an ambulance was on the way. When the cop went to check on Michael's friend, she reached under her skirt, pulled out the wallet, and headed back to her VW bus. That was the last time he ever saw her.

Michael paused in his narrative for a few seconds. "When I was in Casper, I used to cruise around and kick hippies' asses. You know, that's one of the things I regret now. That girl made me love hippies. If I see anybody giving them a hard time now, they have to take me on too. You know what she did? She mailed me my wallet with everything in it, not one dollar missing."

At the hospital Michael gave a phony name. He was bandaged up and left in a room by himself. At the first opportunity, he put on his clothes, climbed out the window, and *hitchhiked* back to New Mexico—my god, would you pick up someone who looked like the mummy hitching a ride on a highway? He made it in time to report to his parole officer with at least fifteen minutes to spare, making up a story to explain his bandaged face.

He was working at a car wash and started a conversation with Ron and Cindy who were trudging along the sidewalk, heading to the edge of town to hitch back to La Perla. As he had mentioned, he loved hippies now. They invited him to come visit, and he took them up on their invitation, and that was when Louie and I ran into him on the road to La Perla.

Michael stayed with Ron and Cindy for a few days, and then left to report to his parole officer. I was sure I would never see him again, but a couple of weeks later he returned. Once again he stayed with Ron and Cindy. He seemed fairly domestic and quiet, helping Ron with a shed he was building, but domesticity and Michael could not be compatible for very long.

On Saturday there was a big picnic party at the swimming hole. About a half-mile outside of town, near the banks of the Rio Grande, was a depression where the water from the water table seeped up and made a pond about thirty yards long and ten wide, and perhaps ten feet deep at its deepest. On this day a number of people from other communities had come and there was lots of food, music, booze and pot, and everybody was skinny dipping. About ten yards from the swimming hole, at the edge of the river was a patch of quicksand. We would step into it and start sinking slowly. It was not like the movies where the bad guy in a pith helmet falls into a pit of quicksand and slowly sinks to a well-deserved death. You would sink down to your waist and then stop. I guess the specific gravity of the soft mud and the human body were equal at that point. The trick was to get out without any help and then run to the swimming hole and jump in and rinse off the gooey mud. It was noisy fun with adults and kids screaming and splashing while Pink Floyd blared in the background.

I remember Cindy, with her large freckled breasts and a shock of red pubic hair, sitting on the plank that had been set up as a diving board, her legs spread, feet paddling in the water. A boy, thirteen, fourteen years old, had gone under water and surfaced between her outspread legs. He remained there, treading water, looking directly at Cindy's red-fringed vagina. It took a few moments before she saw him, kicked water in his face and yelled at him to scram.

"It looks like a picture in *Penthouse Magazine*," he shouted, and everyone erupted in laughter. Except Michael. I noticed him lying on his belly on the sand, looking at Cindy as intently as the boy had. She looked back at him, stood up leisurely, stretched, and slipped into the water. Michael continued watching her for a while, then lay his head down and closed his eyes.

A few days later, late morning, Louie and I were sitting on the old car seat in front of his house, legs thrown out, kicking back, enjoying the morning, when we warped again into a Hollywood movie. Walking down off the mesa, down the center of the road into La Perla, came a young man wearing a black, straight-brimmed hat with a silver *concho* band, a black shirt, black pants, and black cowboy boots with a large, black-handled knife sheathed inside one of the boots, the haft sticking out. Louie's mouth literally dropped open. Here was Jack Palance in *Shane*, only baby-faced. We watched in unbelieving silence as he walked past us toward the pavement's end.

"Oh my God! There's going to be a shoot-out right here in La Perla. Quick, let's go tell John Wayne that Billy the Kid just sauntered into town."

We looked at each other and burst out laughing. Louie trotted after the gunless gunslinger. He had to know who the devil this guy was, and what he was doing on Louie's turf.

When he returned he said, "You're right, the guy does think he's in a B western. The only thing he told me was that he had heard of La Perla in Socorro, and he came down to 'check it out.' He kept squinting like he was near-sighted, but I think he was just trying to look mean."

I found out later that the Kid (he never told us his name) had met Tommy in Socorro, and Tommy, who had an abiding interest in all things bizarre, had invited him to come stay at his place. That night there was a dinner gathering at Ron and Cindy's, and Tommy showed up with his new friend, still in costume, including the big knife in his boot. Michael was there, and he couldn't take his eyes off the Kid. It was clear to me that there was going to be a confrontation between the real cowboy and the wannabe. And sure enough, at one point, Michael stood up and walked over to the Kid.

"That's sure a big knife you got. It's really scary. I'll bet you're good with that knife, huh?" In a blur, Michael's hand reached down and pulled the knife from the Kid's boot. He held it in his hand, turning it over, feeling its heft and balance, and then holding it with the point of the blade aimed at the Kid's gut. "I don't know if I want a scary guy like you carrying such a big knife. Nope. Not a good idea for you to have it. We're all quiet, peaceful people here, and you and this knife are too dangerous for us."

By now everyone in the house was sitting quietly, watching the scene unfold. The Kid looked around gulping, aware that everyone was watching, but he obviously had no idea what to do.

"I want my knife back," he said, not quite plaintively but not far from it either.

Michael laughed. "Why don't you take it back? You're a scary guy, why don't you make me give it back?"

The Kid did nothing, just sat red-faced. Michael turned the knife so the handle pointed at the Kid, and he held it out to him. The Kid reached for it, and Michael pulled it back.

"Say 'pretty please.' Say 'pretty please may I have my knife back'"

The Kid's eyes darted around the room. "Give it to me," he said. His voice now had a slight tremor.

Michael's tone was sharper than the knife. "Take it from me.

You want it, you take it. If you don't take it, I keep it and you walk out of here without a knife."

This clash between reality and illusion was almost painful to watch. For a moment, I thought the Kid was going to cry. Instead he stood and walked out of the house and left La Perla. A few moments later the dinner party was back in full swing and Michael had himself a knife.

Later I saw Michael and Cindy sitting outside on the front porch steps. She had the knife in her hand, holding it delicately.

"Go ahead, keep it," I heard him say.

She giggled. "I'm only five feet tall. What would I do with such a big knife?"

"Well, a big knife can be handy. You just have to know how to use it."

"I bet you know how to use it, don't you?"

Michael did not respond.

You may remember Cindy was from Shaker Heights, the affluent suburb of Cleveland. Her boyfriend Ron was from the lower-income tenement district of Cleveland. They had met at a rock concert, and Cindy's big rebellion against parents and upbringing was to take up with Ron. I guess he was her parents' worst nightmare as far as their hopes for Cindy were concerned. After graduating from high school, they left together in Ron's VW Beetle and headed west in search of a New Mexico commune like the ones they had read about and seen in *Easy Rider*. Instead, they found La Perla.

Eventually she contacted her parents, told them where she was, and they came out from Shaker Heights to try to save their prodigal daughter. When they first saw the adobe house she was living in ("But dear, it's made out of *mud!*"), they were actually afraid to step in, and they hesitated for a few minutes. Cindy finally convinced them that there were no rats, rattlesnakes, or scorpions, and they went inside to try to talk her into returning to Shaker Heights. The harder they tried, the more pleasure Cindy seemed to derive out of denying them their wish. Eventually they left, without Cindy, of course.

Michael was in and out of La Perla. We never knew when he would show up, or why, or how long he would stay. On one of these visits he went to Ron and Cindy's, as usual, to see if he could use their spare room. This time, however, Cindy was alone. Ron had returned to Cleveland to paint his mother's house and would be gone for ten days. Cindy agreed to let Michael use the spare room.

Of course what you think happened, happened. When Ron returned, Michael was still living in his house, but he was no longer sleeping in the spare room. All the freaks had been waiting for Ron's return, wondering how this domestic upheaval was going to play out. It didn't take long to resolve. Michael wanted Cindy, Cindy wanted Michael and Ron, and Ron wanted them both out. Ron won. So much for the sexual revolution and guiltless, non-possessive sex.

Michael and Cindy left quickly, packing a few belongings into Michael's pickup. Now there were two of the original freaks who had left, Cindy and Joel. I heard later that Michael was working as a ranch hand outside of Mountainair, or living on a ranch out by Ladron Peak, or cowboying in Magdalena. Someone saw him and Cindy dancing and whooping at the Cowboy Bar in Pueblitos, having a great time. But without La Perla there was no permanence in their lives, no more home base.

About a year later I heard from Ron that her parents had come to Escondida or Polvadera, or some such place, and this time she agreed to go back to Shaker Heights. Ron remained a bachelor. I never knew where Michael wound up, but I'm sure that wherever it was, there was tumult, excitement, and wild, wild fun.

Industry

After Cindy left La Perla with Michael, Richard, a friend of Louie's from California, came to La Perla and moved into Ron's spare room. Richard promptly began building a house on Ron's property. It was a simple one-room adobe. His girlfriend in San Francisco, where Richard was also from, wanted to escape from the city and come to La Perla, but she refused to move unless he could provide her with a home. The house was about half-finished when Richard ran out of funds.

It was a cool November morning and I was visiting Richard sitting on the front porch of Ron's house, commiserating over our lack of money.

"Well," said Richard, "I guess I have to leave La Perla for a while and get a job. I need cash so I can finish my house. I really want to get Joan here. Gotta get more money. I sure hate to go back to work just for money, but that's life."

"Yeah, money's a bitch. I need money too, but not as much as you. I just need enough to buy an ounce of good pot. Ten bucks is all I want."

"That would be a nice start. I could use some grass myself. There must be a way to make money without having to go into the city, some sort of cottage industry we could have. I keep trying to think of something we can do here in La Perla, but I keep coming up with nothing. I always wind up at the same place: If I want money, I gotta go back into the city."

"How long is Joan willing to wait for you to finish the house?"

"Actually, when I talked to her on the phone two days ago, she was real antsy to come. I think she's about to quit her job in San Francisco and drive here now even though I don't yet have a house. I'm trying to talk her into doing that."

"Let's get back to the important issue. How can we get ten dollars for grass without going into the city to work to get it?"

For the next few days we thought and talked about different projects, some sort of industry that we could use to make us ten dollars apiece. How could we make money when we literally didn't have one cent to invest, had no vehicle, and lived sixty miles from the nearest city? We were rolling the problem around in Ron's kitchen when Ron came in and went straight to the sink and started scrubbing his hands. Suddenly the kitchen was filled with the aroma of forest and mountain.

"I was walking out on the mesa," Ron said, "and I sat under a juniper tree for a while and wound up with this sap from the tree all over my hand. Boy is it hard to get off."

Suddenly it hit me. Our cottage industry! We wanted to buy some weed; traditionally, what went with smoking dope? "Incense!" I said.

"Huh?" said Richard.

"We make juniper incense and we sell it! It doesn't cost any money to get the materials. We just have Ron here go sit naked under juniper trees, and then we scrape the sap off him, make incense, and sell it. *Voila!* Ten dollars apiece."

"You're crazy," was Ron's assessment.

But the more Richard and I talked about the possibility of making incense, the more excited we got.

"But how do we market it?" wondered Richard, who had majored in Business Administration in college. "Do we go door-to-door? I mean, a middle-class housewife answers the door and here's a couple of hippies selling incense. 'Please Ma'am, would you help two destitute freaks by buying some incense so they can get a lid of marijuana'?"

"Ha! I got the marketing angle all figured out. In two weeks the University of New Mexico is holding an annual arts and crafts fair in the ballroom of the Student Union. I know a lady who makes quilts, and she's rented a booth at the fair to sell them. I bet she would let us use a corner of her booth to sell incense at no cost. We could make twenty dollars easy."

And so the Great Intergalactic Incense Company was born. We quickly got the Research and Development Department up and running. The first problem was pretty basic: How do we make incense? Neither of us had the foggiest notion.

We started by collecting sap. Ron refused to help us by sitting naked under juniper trees and letting sap collect on him, so we had to come up with another method of harvesting the sap. It was not easy. It stuck to anything it touched, was next to impossible to remove, and it didn't burn worth a damn. We then tried juniper needles. We stripped needles off the trees on the mesa, took them to Ron's house, and tried making different concoctions. We ran them through a small mill-grinder attached to Ron's kitchen table, producing an odiferous green mush which we then placed on a cookie sheet and let sit in a warm oven for a couple of hours. This resulted in a green powder which was highly aromatic when burned, but it burned much too quickly. In fact, it flashburned—a miniature explosion and a cloud of lovely-smelling smoke.

After a week of working on the problem, R&D came up with a solution. We determined that if we took the dry, powdered juniper needles, mixed them with a smidgen of sap so the powder cohered, and then shaped the mix into one-inch cones and placed them in a warm oven for a while, we got an aromatic cone that didn't stick to our fingers, and smoldered for about fifteen minutes when lit. And I do mean aromatic. Our incense brought the forest into the house.

Now the Intergalactic Incense Company shifted from research to full-scale Production mode. We had five days before the fair, and we were working overtime using Ron's kitchen for the assembly line. The first day of production we had a visitor. Willie, the town drunk and ne'er-do-well from one of the original La Perla families, dropped in to observe our operation.

"I hear you're starting a bakery," he slurred.

"Oh? Where'd you hear that, Willie?" asked Richard.

"Everybody in La Perla and Concepcion is talking about the bakery that's opening up here. I came to try some of your bread."

"Our company's not in the Retailing mode yet, Willie," said Richard. "We've just started Production." We had one cookie sheet baking in the oven and another with cones that were finished and cooling on the table.

"That's funny looking bread," said Willie as he picked up one of the cones and examined it. "It's green. How come you make such small loaves? Is it health bread? Give me a loaf, and if it's good bread I'll tell everyone in La Perla and Concepcion, and you'll sell it all."

"It's incense, Willie," said Richard.

"Oh. What kind of bread is that?" Willie took the cone in his hand and popped it into his mouth. He munched it silently while Richard and I stared at each other. He swallowed and announced, "That's pretty good bread. I'll let everybody know." He stood up and lurched out the door.

"By God," said Richard, "we may be on to something here. Edible incense. Wonder if there's a market for that?"

"We could sell it as aromatic bread *and* edible incense both. This could be big, *really* big."

By the day before the arts and crafts fair, the Intergalactic Incense Company, Production Division, had produced enough incense to turn over to the Retail Division. Richard and I hitchhiked to Albuquerque, stayed overnight with friends, then headed to the University the next morning. Deborah was already in the ballroom setting up her quilts when we arrived. It seemed like there were already hundreds of vendors ready to sell their goods. We set our incense stock in a corner of Deborah's booth next to a hand-lettered sign: "Plato's Incense! Ideal! None better! Incense of the gods!"

"I hope the two of us can handle the business," said Richard. "Hope we don't get swamped."

I wandered around the Ballroom and saw that many booths were selling incense. Damn near every booth had sticks or cones burning. I reported to Richard.

"Lots of competition, man. Lots of incense."

"Let's show 'em what real incense smells like."

He took one of our demo cones and lit it. In a few minutes the entire ballroom smelled like a juniper forest on a cool summer morning. People were actually going around looking and asking for the source of the aroma, looking specifically for our product. In less than an hour we had sold all twenty of our packets for a dollar each. Rarely have businessmen, no matter how enterprising, achieved such total success so rapidly.

"You know," said Richard, "maybe we ought to consider going into business on a larger scale."

"I dunno. I'm kinda wary about that. I don't think I want to go into the world of commerce real heavy. I mean, we worked on this project for almost two weeks. Two weeks of pressure, pressure, pressure. Stress like that can't be good for you. Business is too heavy duty for my blood.

"And besides, too much money's not good for the soul. Root of all evil and so forth. And will we be satisfied with making ten bucks each every two or three weeks? No way! We're going to want more, twenty, or maybe even thirty dollars. Apiece! And then we'll wind up spending all our time grubbing for money. I say we shut the operation down, take the money and run to our nearest friendly dealer for some grass."

"Yeah, I guess you're right. It's not good for the spirit. Already the business mentality was corrupting me, making me greedy. Ten dollars wasn't enough. I wanted more, and more. You're right: too much risk."

We split the twenty bucks, found our contact in town, and bought two ounces of marijuana. Richard stayed in town while I hitchhiked back to La Perla, always an adventure in itself. I got dropped off in Veguita, about fifteen miles from La Perla, so I stopped in to say hi to a young lady I had met the week before. She was gracious, accommodating, and agreeable. We smoked some of my dope, and my visit took up most of the afternoon. She gave me her loving and a pair of boots that were too large for her, good boots, Spanish boots of Spanish leather. I continued hitchhiking feeling like the king of the world.

As I entered La Perla riding in the back of a pickup, I thought about the Great Intergalactic Incense Company and its amazing success. Perhaps I had missed my calling. Perhaps the world of business *was* where I belonged. The Emperor of Incense. But who wants to spend his time doing the same thing over and over? And there was the whole corrupting profit/money angle. Definitely best to jump in and get out fast, take the money and run. Always best to quit when you're ahead.

And so the Great Intergalactic Incense Company went belly-up while at the very pinnacle of success. The hard-driving life of the big-time incense magnate couldn't hold a candle to the Country Gentleman's life of ease.

Voices

Kyle drove me back to La Perla after I had spent a few days visiting him and Deborah at their farmhouse forty miles north of La Perla. We decided to stop at Louie's, and when we went in through the kitchen door without knocking, we walked in on a young woman sitting naked in a tin tub of hot water. Startled, she leaped up looking for a towel to wrap around herself, but there was none within reach. So she stood, like Venus rising, one arm across her breasts, the other shielding her crotch.

She looked at us for a moment, then shrugged and dropped her arms to her sides. "What the hell. You've already had a good look at me. Would one of you please hand me that towel?"

I grabbed it and handed it to her.

She wrapped it around herself casually. "Are you Raf?"

"Yeah. Sorry to bust in on you. This is Kyle. Is Louie here?"

"He's at Joel's. I'm Karen, a friend of Richard's. And Louie's friend now." She held out her hand in greeting. When she did, a corner of the towel dropped, exposing her left breast. We shook hands as she laughed. "I can't stand here naked making small talk. Excuse me but I have to get dressed."

She turned clutching the towel to her front, revealing her bare bottom as she walked out of the kitchen.

I grinned at Kyle. "You sure got a nice La Perla welcome."

"Oh my. If I weren't married I'd be moving down here tomorrow. Sex, drugs, and rock and roll."

"You know it aint like it looks. The sex isn't as free and

wild as people think, and drugs are too expensive. Nobody here grows any pot. Too dangerous."

Karen came out fully dressed. "I'm a friend of Richard's and Joan's from San Francisco. Joan decided to come live here and help Richard finish building a home for them. I came just to get away from work for a few days. Louie says I can stay here while I'm visiting."

Yeah, I'll bet you can. Louie's no dummy. She was attractive, slender with curly, dark blonde hair, grey-green eyes, smallish breasts, and large hips and ass. But what struck me was her voice. She had one of the sexiest voices I had ever heard. She wasn't trying to sound sexy; it was just her natural voice, and it made a taut cord in me vibrate. I was attracted to her as I had not been attracted to a woman in a long time.

"She's your *anima*," Kyle told me when I discussed my situation with him. "Jung says men have a feminine aspect which is a basic part of their make-up. The *anima* in a man represents the archetypal woman, or what a man, deep down in his unconscious mind thinks a woman—with a capital W—should be. When a man meets a woman who reflects these archetypes for him, he is very attracted to her. Something in her triggers this response in you."

"Her voice. I hear her voice and I'm immediately turned on. Is that how Jung defines love, a response to the *anima*?"

"That's part of it. Men do tend to fall in love with women who reflect their *anima*."

"I don't know that I'd call it love, but she sure stimulates something in me. Could just be lust. 'The twitching of three abdominal nerves,' Pound called it. Maybe that's all she does for me, twitch those nerves. I can look at this woman rationally and think that I really don't need her very much, but once she talks to me, I want her, and I want her now."

Kyle chuckled. "Once you get into sex and love, you can forget about reason and logic. Your *anima* is in control."

"I read somewhere that Aristotle once fell for a young woman, probably a maid in Alexander the Great's court. She would supposedly make him get down on all fours and then she'd ride him like a pony. God, can you imagine that? The greatest mind of his time, one of the greatest minds of all time, playing horsey? If his *anima* could do that to him, what chance do I have?"

"Yeah, it's tricky. This man-woman-sex stuff is dynamite. Nothing you can do except try to keep stable, maintain some control, and hope for the best. Not easy."

I thought, *Yes, this anima business is pretty strong stuff.*

Karen's visit extended from a few days to a few weeks, and then talk of her returning to San Francisco ended. She was now one of the permanent resident freaks of La Perla. She and Louie were now a couple.

Not long after, Karen became pregnant. All the freaks in town were excited over her pregnancy. This would be the first freak child born in La Perla, a milestone of sorts. Donna, a registered midwife from Concepcion, made regular visits checking on Karen's progress. As she swelled bigger and bigger, the women in La Perla and Concepcion bustled around her, bringing food, doing house chores, and taking charge of Louie's household in general.

I had heard that women take on a "radiance" when they get pregnant, but I had never seen this. Pregnant women always looked grotesque and awkward with that impossibly huge belly and the clumsy struggle to go from the horizontal to the vertical, and the leaning-back waddle that substituted for a normal walk. In Karen, I saw it for the first time. She did look radiant even in the most mundane or unpleasant situations. One morning I was standing at a window of my house when I saw the kitchen door of Louie's open, and Karen, about six months pregnant, staggered out. She was dressed in a green, flowing robe with gold trim, and

I caught my breath at her beauty. She stood there for a moment, then sticking out her hand, she leaned against the house and proceeded to throw up. But even then, from my window she looked *radiant* in her forest green gown.

A Birth

As Karen got bigger and bigger there was an increasing air of excitement among all of us. Having a birth was taken as an affirmation that we freaks were in La Perla for the long haul. We were as solicitous toward Karen as if we were members of a close-knit family, and we felt that, in a sense, we had a proprietary interest in the coming babe. Karen had decided on a home birth, and even though she made regular trips to the clinic in Socorro for check-ups, she was also under the care of Donna, a practicing midwife from Concepcion who provided Karen with almost daily checks on her condition.

Louie, however, seemed to be in shock at the idea of being a father. Louie could be something of a space cowboy, drifting off into his own world on occasion, but as the due date approached, his distraction increased, and he walked around talking to himself more than usual. But fatherhood, even impending fatherhood, brought new responsibilities and obligations. He had the responsibility of seeing that his car, a tumble-down English Rover, was in good running condition at all times in case there should be an emergency requiring a hasty trip to the hospital in Socorro, some thirty miles away. He began disassembling and reassembling various parts of the engine, carefully cleaning and lubricating whatever needed lubricating and cleaning, and replacing parts which seemed to need replacing. I had never seen Louie so organized and methodical.

Every day he would test some aspect of the car: headlights,

tail lights, brake lights, replacing bulbs and wires, tooting the horn, putting in new brake fluid and an oil filter, and on and on. I was impressed. This was a new Louie to me. I would often see him leaning over a fender, the hood upraised, listening intently to the idling engine while mumbling to himself. Sometimes, after some minor repair or modification, the engine would not start. Louie would then stomp away and leave the car with the hood up and his tools scattered around it, and wander the mesa for an hour or two mumbling incoherently. Then back to the Rover he would go, with new determination and more cleaning, lubricating, replacing, and modifying. Finally, a few days before Karen's due date, Louie announced that the car was ready, or at least as ready as he could make it. He could think of nothing else to do to it.

Karen's contractions started a few nights later, at around three in the morning. In a final test of his car, Louie raced to Concepcion to get the midwife and bring her to La Perla.

By sun up, all the freaks knew that Karen was in labor. Every freak in town was soon in Louie's house trying to help, but in general just getting in the way. Karen lay in bed, the midwife beside her coaching her on her breathing while Karen panted and groaned. The freaks gathered in the living room and in the yard. By early afternoon she was exhausted, but the recalcitrant baby was still refusing to cooperate. Eventually, tired of lying in bed, Karen came into the living room and sat on a pillow, leaning back against the wall, knees bent, legs spread, nightgown bunched up around her waist. The freaks formed a cheering section, shouting encouragement whenever she groaned and pushed. "Atta girl! Come on Karen! Push, push, push!" But baby remained stubborn.

Karen was sweating, wan and disheveled, her head drooping down. "Jesus, I am so tired."

"Hey," said Richard, "I got an idea. Why don't you smoke a joint and see if that helps you relax and push."

"OK," said Karen, "I'm ready to try anything."

"A little hippie medicine," said Ron.

"I got an even better idea," added Richard. "Why don't we *all* smoke some grass and our combined vibes will attract the baby and it'll pop right out."

"A little hippie philosophy," said Ron.

The group consensus was that Richard had a grand idea, and soon several joints were circulating. Karen sat on the floor against the wall, toking and pushing, her damp hair drooping limply against her sweaty forehead. She looked up at the crowd around her and managed a half-smile.

"God, this is embarrassing. Sitting here with no underpants and my legs spread out in front of a whole bunch of people." She paused, and then pushed and groaned again. "The baby's not coming out, but I *am* getting stoned."

Donna, the midwife was increasingly concerned. "For whatever reason the baby is not coming out. We should go to the hospital," she said. "Do you want to go?" she asked Karen.

"Yes, yes. I can't do this any longer."

"Well, the car's ready to go," said Louie with a touch of pride.

Suddenly everyone was in motion. Two men were helping Karen stand up, someone was grabbing an overnight bag, and Louie was running outside to start the car.

"Boil some water!" shouted Richard. "They always boil water in the movies when babies are born. It's an ancient tribal thing."

"Shut up and stay out of the way," said Donna.

Then we were all outside cheering as the car sped toward Socorro carrying Louie, Karen, and Donna.

"Maybe we oughta follow them," said Joel to Sara, "in case something goes wrong." They got into Joel's antique Volvo and left a few minutes after the Rover.

At this point, Murphy awoke and thought *It's time to put my law into action*. . . .

Later, Louie told me what happened after they left La Perla. He had taken care of every aspect of getting his car ready for an emergency, save one: He had forgotten to put gas in the car. So halfway to Socorro they ran out of gas. With the car stranded on the highway and Karen groaning and moaning in the back seat, Donna lost her cool. She jumped out of the vehicle and ran out into the middle of the interstate waving her arms frantically. A semi managed to screech to a stop a few feet before it ran into her, and Donna climbed into the cab shouting, "There's a baby having a woman in that car! They're out of gas! I have to get to a gas station!" And off they roared.

The trucker dropped her off at the first gas station a few miles up the road, and Donna ran in. Jabbering in her excitement, she had to convince the station manager that there really was a woman having a baby in the back seat of a car five miles up the road. Once he began to accept that as true, she realized that in her haste she had forgotten her purse in the back seat of the Rover. She then had to convince the owner to *lend* her a gas can so she could take some gas back to the car. She promised she would return later and pay for the gas can and the gas. At this the manager balked.

"Yeah, right. How about some sandwiches and a bottle of pop too, and anything else you like."

"Please, please. This is an emergency! We have to get Karen to the hospital!"

The manager stood with arms crossed, not moving and saying nothing. Donna whirled, grabbed a gas can off a shelf and waved it wildly in the manager's face, shouting "Damnit! Give me some gas!"

"All right, all right," the frightened manager said, backing up a few paces. "I'll lend you the can, but you damn sure better bring it back."

"I'll pay you for the damned thing, just hurry!"

After filling the can, the manager asked for a dollar-ten for the gas.

"You don't understand, I don't have any money with me. My purse is in the car."

"No money, no gas."

"Oh shit! I'll pay you your damned money and bring back your can, but I have to get that woman to a hospital!" With that she jerked the can out of the manager's hands, turned and ran out to the highway, leaving the manager standing by the gas pump.

"I'll call the cops!" he shouted after her.

Donna quickly flagged down another vehicle which took her back to the Rover. She jumped out and ran to the car. It was empty—no Karen, no Louie, no baby. She stood there perplexed, holding her can of gasoline. *They must have hitched a ride to Socorro! Surely a woman in labor would have no trouble hitching a ride.* Leaving the gas in the back seat, she almost got smashed flagging down another vehicle. She got to hospital twenty minutes after the baby had been born. A little boy. Mother, baby, and father were all fine, but Donna was a nervous wreck.

That night we had a celebration in La Perla for mother and child, *in absentia*, since they were still in the hospital. There was champagne and pot for everyone, and we all agreed that, all in all, it had been a pretty smooth birth.

Commitment

Now in La Perla decisions were being made, events were happening, all more or less without my active participation. I enjoyed thinking of myself as unattached, free, but the reality was that everyone else still saw Jill and me as a couple. Ultimately it seemed easier to go with the flow than to swim against it. So we moved in together.

For six months we had shared her house, and I was still learning how to adapt to her rhythms and her explosive moods. I learned to take cover from those explosions. People who knew Jill slightly saw her public persona—quiet, unassuming, the type of person who could be easily pushed around. In actuality she was as mushy as a bag of nails. Her way of dealing with disagreement and dissension was confrontation, immediate and aggressive, with shouting and broken crockery; my way was avoidance, pulling in my head and drawing into my shell. Sometimes we would go days without speaking to each other. It was an awful lot like my marriage had been.

But this day Jill had left for Kansas to visit her family and childhood friends, and I was single again. Early in the afternoon I wandered over to Ron's house and noticed a Dodge Dart, a car I had not seen in La Perla before, parked in front of his house. Ron, Richard, Tommy, and an attractive dark-haired woman were sitting on Ron's front porch. The men were animated, talking and laughing loudly while the woman sat watching, obviously amused.

Ron introduced her as Mary, from Los Angeles. She and her

five-year-old son had picked Ron up hitchhiking on the Interstate, and having nothing better to do, brought him to La Perla. When I shook her hand, she looked in my eyes and smiled.

"There are lots of places in La Perla where you can stay," Ron was saying. "Most of the houses have extra rooms. My house has a spare bedroom, and you and Robbie are welcome to stay here."

"I don't know if we're going to stay. I have to ask Robbie how he feels."

"Joel and Sara are gone for a few weeks," I said. "You could stay in their house."

"I don't know. Maybe."

I stood on Ron's porch watching the excited bachelors maneuver for position with her like watching a horse race in which no horse seemed able to break away from the pack, or like watching kids cavorting and shouting "Look at me!"

I expressed my pleasure at meeting Mary and headed back to Jill's house, listening to the competing men on Ron's porch, the note of excitement coming through even as the voices grew weaker. I paced around Jill's house (I never thought of it as *my* house too) waiting for what I was sure was going to happen. Sometimes I have a prescience about women. After about an hour there was a knock on the door.

It was Mary and a small boy whom she introduced as Robbie. She had decided to stay in Joel's house, and was wondering if I had any milk for Robbie. I gave her a quart from the fridge, and as she turned to leave, she asked if I wanted to have dinner with her and Robbie. Naturally I accepted. I stood in the doorway watching her liquid motion as she sauntered away in her granny skirt, holding Robbie's hand. *The liquefaction of her clothes.* I almost rubbed my hands in anticipation and glee, like some evil villain in a cheap movie, about to ravish the innocent heroine.

I don't remember what she made for dinner; I wasn't paying much attention even as I ate. Robbie carried on most of the conversation while Mary and I nodded or grunted, not really listening. I thought of the scene in the film *Tom Jones* where the hero and a woman are sitting at table slurping oysters and sipping wine as a prelude to going to bed. I kept waiting for Robbie to finish and go out to play.

After he went out, Mary and I sat and talked. She was straightforward and immediately mentioned that the other guys had told her that I was part of a couple. I felt a surge of anger at the guys for even mentioning Jill, but of course that was part of their jockeying for position with Mary. I assumed that my chances of bedding Mary were gone.

"Are you two real tight?" she asked.

I hesitated, thinking of an answer that would be true, but evasive. "We've been together six months. I guess it's like most couples: Sometimes it's nice and smooth, and other times you wonder why you bother staying together."

She dropped the subject and started talking about herself. She had separated from her live-in boyfriend, Robbie's father, three years earlier, and she and Robbie had been scraping by since. She had waitressed, clerked in a clothing store, even picked fruit to stay alive.

"The last job I had was in a 'massage parlor' in Los Angeles." She looked at me intently as she said this. "It was the best-paying job I've had since James and I separated. I worked there about five months. The only time I've been able to save some money in three years. I quit a week ago."

I imagined her at work as a *masseuse*, a pornographic reel I ran in my mind, and my desire level rose. "Why did you quit?"

"I liked the money, but I was tired of not having any control. You know, some asshole comes in and he's got fifty bucks, so like it or not. . . ." She shrugged. "And Robbie's getting old enough that I was worried he'd tell the teachers in kindergarten about the 'day care' where mommy worked, or he'd figure out what mommy did, and I just didn't want that hassle. Does it bother you?"

"Does what bother me?"

"What I was doing, working in one of those parlors."

"No, not really."

She laughed. "It turns you on, doesn't it? I can tell."

She stood up and walked to me and stood between my knees. She put her arms around my head, drawing me to her breasts, pressing my face against her softness.

"Oooh." she moaned lowly. "Baby I really want you. I haven't had sex for fun with a man in months." She tilted my head up so I was looking at her. "You're thinking of all the nasty things I did and that you want to do with me." She laughed again. "You get the 'Special,' and you get it free."

The door flung open and she stepped back. Robbie ran in breathless from running around on the mesa. "Mom, mom! I can see the whole town from up there! There's a bunch of sheep that some dogs are bringing into town, and you can hear the sheep going baaa and the dogs barking, and it's really neat!"

She smiled at him. "That's nice, Robbie. Go wash up and get ready for bed. I'll lie down with you until you go to sleep."

When Robbie was ready she went with him into the next room and lay down with him. I could hear them whispering for a while, and then there was silence. She came out of the other room naked. In the soft flickering light of the kerosene lantern her body was golden, with a rush of dark hair falling over one shoulder, and the mysterious, dark triangle between her thighs. I was sitting on the bed, still clothed, and she pushed me back, pressing her mouth on mine.

It was hot, sweaty, summer lovemaking which ended with the sheet on the floor and the two of us entangled and exhausted. I awoke at midmorning, the sun already high and the room warming. I was alone in bed, and then Mary came in from Robbie's room.

"I was checking to see if Robbie was awake, but I guess he's already running around outside." She giggled. "I was so knocked out I never heard him." She got back into bed. "Let's do that again."

She was lying on top of me when Robbie came running in.

She pulled the sheet over us without disengaging. He ran to the bedside telling his mom he was hungry while she lay on me, resting her weight on her elbows.

"Robbie," she said, "there's some fruit on the table. Why don't you take some and go outside and play, and in a little while I'll make you breakfast."

"OK." He ran into the kitchen, and then we heard the front door slam. We had both been lying completely still, and when Robbie left, she laughed, and then moved urgently, grinding slowly against me.

After lovemaking and breakfast, I went back to Jill's and slept for a few more hours. I was weeding the garden that afternoon when Mary came by. Ron had taken Robbie for a hike in the desert, and they wouldn't be back for hours. We went inside and made love again.

The women I had been with the last few years had been "strong, independent feminists," and often lovemaking had the feel of a struggle, a determined search for some common ground a man and woman could meet on. There was little of the mutual submission I had always associated with lovemaking. Mary was strong and independent, but she gave her body easily and willingly, a source of joy and pleasure. It was wonderful to have *passion* in my love life again. When she went back to Joel and Sara's, I was exhausted but not satiated, and I kept thinking of how easy it was to be with her, even when we weren't in bed.

We continued as lovers for a week, and on the day Jill was due back we were lying in bed at midmorning. Mary knew Jill was returning and we both assumed this was our last time together. This time it was different.

"Don't worry," Mary said. "I'm not stepping in between you two." But while we were making love I kept thinking of Jill arriving and finding us in bed, and the outburst that would come with that. I had difficulty achieving orgasm, and afterward we lay on our backs, only our fingers touching.

I wanted to hold her and plead with her not to go, or to tell her that I would go with her, that we were great together, but the image of Jill screaming and throwing things that would come with my leaving her kept me bottled. Maybe the whole situation would be taken out of my hands. Maybe Jill would stay in Kansas, or maybe she would come back and break off our relationship since it wasn't working. Then I could leave with Mary and Robbie easily and smoothly.

Robbie! I could not imagine myself taking responsibility for a child. The fantasy of leaving with Mary began to crumble.

Mary rolled over on her side, facing me. "Robbie is the most important person in my life," she said, as if she read my mind. "He's my first concern in everything I do."

"Yeah, he's a nice kid."

"He's a great kid. He's my best friend. I would never do anything to separate us or hurt him."

"What are you planning to do? You can stay here in La Perla. We could find you guys a house."

"I don't think so. That would be too uncomfortable for both of us. Ron was telling me about a place on the back road to Santa Fe, an old ghost town that freaks are moving into and turning into a community again. I was thinking of going there and seeing what that's like."

"Madrid?"

"Yeah, that was the name."

We lay quiet for a few minutes. "It must be nice to have a strong commitment to another person who's not your child," she said. "I really miss that. Jill's lucky." She sat up. "I better get dressed and get my stuff together. I wouldn't want Jill to come and catch us screwing behind her back." She kissed me lightly and got up.

Jill arrived a couple of hours later. I heard her VW bus roll in and was mired in a swamp of regret and frustration. She was so happy to be back in La Perla. She ran to me and hugged, and I hugged her back. She talked excitedly about her trip, telling me how strange it was to be back in her childhood bedroom, and seeing old friends who had not changed a bit, and how well her parents were doing. I gave an occasional grunt to let her know I was listening.

Later we walked down the street so she could see her friends in town. As we walked past Joel and Sara's house, I saw Mary and Robbie putting the last of their stuff in her car. We stopped and I introduced them to Jill.

"You're so lucky to be able to live here," said Mary to Jill. "You must be very happy to be back."

Jill and I turned and walked to Louie's house. "It's so good to be back home and to be with you again," she confided, giving me a little girl's smile.

As we entered Louie's yard I looked back and saw the Dodge Dart going up the mesa and away. It wasn't long before I was spending more and more time at my house and less at Jill's.

House with hour glass I   Photo courtesy of Bob Christensen

Law West of the Rio Grande

Bernardo Romero was from one of the original families in La Perla. He served in the Army during WWII, and like so many others in town, left a few months after the War ended. He too moved to California, to Barstow, where he worked as an accountant for the Santa Fe Railroad. Unlike the other young men who left La Perla after the War and never came back, some twenty-five years later he returned to La Perla with his family after retiring. He built a yellow brick California-style ranch house, the only non-adobe house in La Perla. It stood out like a throbbing thumb smashed by a hammer. The freaks all thought the house was grotesquely ugly and should have stayed in California.

Bernardo now raised pigs and grew alfalfa as a cash crop. He was not happy when he returned and found that half of the residents in La Perla were freaks. The freaks were not part of his memory of what La Perla had been like before the War, and he wanted us out. He and Federico Baca were the only old timers who openly despised the freaks and refused to speak to us or even acknowledge our existence. But Federico Baca disliked everyone, not just the freaks, and he treated everyone, including Bernardo and other old-timers, with equal disdain.

Bernardo's property abutted the back yard of the house that Jill was renting from Solario Canutillo, who lived in Las Cruces over 150 miles away. The house was really dilapidated when she rented it, and she and the freaks had spent days fixing it up. It was now a tight, secure house, Jill's home, though I still came and went.

One day, when Jill was in Socorro doing errands and buying supplies, Bernardo extended the barbed wire fence that enclosed his property past his boundary line and around Solario Canutillo's property, thereby enclosing Jill's house in the process, as if her house were now his property. When Jill came home, Bernardo and his helper had just finished putting up the fence and were almost done installing a gate wide enough for Bernardo to drive his pickup through and have access to his pasture behind Jill's house.

Jill jumped out of her VW bus and confronted him. "What are you doing?" she shouted. "You can't put up a fence here, it's not your property."

He totally ignored her, not responding to anything she said, not even with a grunt. Jill stood with her fists clenched at her sides debating whether she should attack him, but then realized that was probably the worst thing she could do. So she just stood and watched, so frustrated she could not speak. They finished the gate and Bernardo padlocked it. He did not offer Jill a key to the lock. Now the only access to her house was through a locked gate to which she had no key. To get to her house, she, and any visitors, now had to climb over the gate, which presented problems if she had groceries or any large items to carry.

There was no way Jill was going to take this without a fight.

She searched for days before she managed to contact Solario in Las Cruces. No, he said, he had not given Bernardo permission to fence in his property. Would Solario send her a notarized statement to that effect? Yes, he would, and did. In the meanwhile, Jill and her friends had to continue climbing over the gate.

The next time she saw Bernardo unlocking his gate she ran up to him waving the document from Solario. She read it to him and demanded that he remove the fence and the gate so that she could have access to the house she had rented from the legal owner. Again, Bernardo ignored her, and ostentatiously snapped the padlock shut and drove off, leaving Jill in his dust, Solario's statement in her hand.

Jill was not a woman to take an insult lightly. The next time she saw Bernardo he was on horseback riding up to the gate. Before he dismounted she was out the door running to the gate. Once again she demanded that he remove the fence and gate, and once again he completely ignored her. But this time Jill was prepared to escalate the war. She pulled a pair of wire cutters from her back pocket, and looking Bernardo in the eye, began cutting the barb wire of his fence.

This time he did not ignore her. At first he was speechless, and then he exploded.

"You can't cut my fence!"

"I just did."

Bernardo was turning purple. "If you were a man I'd show you what happens to fence cutters!"

"If *you* were a man I wouldn't have to be cutting your fence."

"I'll take you to court and make you pay for this!"

So Jill went to court, the magistrate court in Socorro. All the freaks in La Perla went with her in a caravan of several beat up old cars to watch blind Lady Justice at work. Figuring she had an incontestable right of access to her house, Jill represented herself in court and came with Solario's notarized statement.

The freaks all sat down and waited in stifling heat for court to begin. The magistrate walked in, a wizened old man who had been magistrate in Socorro since New Mexico was a territory over fifty years ago, and still thought of himself as the only true legal authority in Socorro County. We all rose, sat back down, and court was in session.

Bernardo and Jill stood before the bench side by side. Bernardo presented his case first.

"Your Honor, on Tuesday, May 12, I was about to open the

gate in my fence in La Perla, when this"—here he paused and pointed to Jill—"*woman* came running and shouting and cut my fence right in front of me."

The magistrate leaned forward in astonishment. "What? Are you saying she *cut your fence?!*"

"Yes your Honor. She cut it right in front of me."

The magistrate turned to Jill. "Young lady, did you cut this man's fence?"

"Yes, your Honor. He had fenced in my. . . ."

"Wait a minute!" the magistrate interrupted. "Out West you never cut a man's fence! Why, that's like shooting a man's dog, or his wife. No honest, decent person ever does that. You must pay this man the cost of repairing his fence and twenty-five dollars court costs." Glaring at Jill he slammed his gavel hard on the courtroom desk. "Case dismissed. Next."

"But your Honor. . . ."

"Case dismissed! Next."

Jill turned and looked at us freaks in disbelief. The participants in the next case were shuffling around waiting for her to leave. Joel walked up to her and put his hand on her shoulder. "Come on Jilly. It's time to go."

And so the wheels of Justice turned. Solario in Las Cruces refused to go through the hassle of pressing charges against Bernardo, and Jill and her friends continued climbing over the gate. But the Lord moves in mysterious and inefficient ways, and Jill eventually got her revenge and her access.

A few weeks after the magistrate's decision, La Perla got hit by a cloudburst. The heavenly gates opened and the torrents came pouring down. The run-off roared down from the East Mesa, turning main street into a river rushing down Jill's driveway, past her house and into Bernardo's pasture behind her house. Since the pasture was the low spot of the property, it quickly became a lake about three feet deep. Bernardo had left his pigs and the little piglets in the pasture while he and his family had gone out, and now they were struggling to keep from drowning.

When Jill heard the pigs squealing in terror she went out and saw them thrashing about in the water deep enough to drown the piglets. She crawled through the fence and carried the piglets, about thirty pounds apiece, one at a time to higher ground in the driving rain. She then went back into the water to push and pull some of the panicked adult pigs to safety. As luck—or Justice— would have it, Bernardo and his family drove up just as Jill was saving the last of the pigs. There she stood, exhausted, clothes drenched and muddied, hair plastered against her forehead, gasping for breath while Bernardo mumbled embarrassed thanks.

Afterwards, the freaks thought Bernardo would relent and at least unlock his damned gate. But Bernardo was a tough cookie. He made no offer of reconciliation and continued behaving toward Jill as if she did not exist. Days passed and the gate remained in place, still locked. About a week after the rain, Bernardo's wife, Luisa, came to Jill's house with a bag of freshly baked *biscochitos* in gratitude for the rescue of their pigs. Jill watched through the window as Luisa stood at the gate for a few moments. Obviously she did not have a key to the lock. Looking all around to make sure no one was watching and visibly steeling herself, this middle-aged matron squared her shoulders, hiked up her skirts, and took on the undignified task of climbing over the gate. Once over the gate, she looked around again, to make sure no one had witnessed her loss of dignity. She spent the afternoon visiting with Jill, eating *biscochitos* and drinking coffee. When she left, she had to climb over the cursed gate again.

The next day, Bernardo came and quietly and sheepishly removed the lock from the gate. He said not a word to Jill, and he and Jill never became friends, never talked to each other, but that damned gate was never locked again.

House with hour glass II   Photo courtesy of Bob Christensen

Feast!

Louie and Tommy were sitting on what had once been the back seat of a car but which was now an outdoor couch leaning against the south side of Louie's house. It was early March, a clear, sunny morning that obligated me to join them on the seat, legs spread out straight in front of me, soaking up the warmth, the house protecting us from the March winds.

"The Spring Equinox is coming," said Tommy lazily. Winter's ending, time for a celebration."

"That's right! We gotta start getting ready for the Equinox Feast." Louie was sitting up, excited. "Time to start thinking about the food and getting some musicians together. Spring! It's time to get moving again!"

"I'm going to Socorro tomorrow," said Tommy. "I'll talk to Larry Porter, see what musicians he knows that will come play at a party."

"I'll go to Albuquerque and check with musicians there. We should talk to the freaks here and see what food we can get together," Louie added. "Ah man, Spring!"

Every year the freaks in La Perla had a celebration on the Spring equinox and on Thanksgiving Day. These were the two major social events of the year in La Perla. In a sense the two feast days were an affirmation of what we, in an inchoate and inarticulate manner, were trying to do—create a sense of community and sharing within a larger society which, because of its very size, did not easily allow for closeness. We had to *make* our own community. These feast days were a way of saying to the outside world, "See, it is possible for people to live together, cooperate, and enjoy each other's company." At any rate, on those days it always seemed to me that people envied us for this closeness that they too wanted but had not yet been able to achieve in their daily lives. People saw us at a time of joy and celebration, but were unaware of the constant adaptations, explanations, compromises, frustrations, and adjustments that went with living closely within a diverse group. Such is the price of community.

Preparations for the Equinox party began weeks in advance. We would contact local musicians in Socorro to the south and Albuquerque to the north and invite them to come and play—for free of course. We freaks would pool our money for a couple of turkeys and kegs of beer, and each household would begin planning for the dishes it would make. News of the party spread through the underground grapevine, not only in Socorro and Albuquerque, but throughout tiny communities like Concepcion, *Bosque*, Polvadera, Escondida, Veguita, and La Nutrias, each of which had its small contingent of freaks, and word spread even as far north as Taos and Dixon, in the highlands of New Mexico one hundred fifty miles away.

As the party date drew nearer, the freaks in La Perla got more and more excited. The day before the party, everyone was antsy and giggly, like kids on Christmas Eve. We were about to see more people than we had seen since the last party months before. For the single men this meant the arrival of unattached women, and there was always the hope that one of these ladies would want to stay in La Perla permanently.

The Equinox Feast began in the evening with music, dancing, drinking, and marijuana smoking, and it went on all night. The Thanksgiving Feast was more of a daytime, contemplative affair centered around dinner. On Thanksgiving, folks would begin arriving in the late morning, and soon there were kids screaming and running around town playing in the ruined and dying houses. Informal expeditions would set out to explore the desert on the mesa and maybe find an obsidian arrowhead or two in what had once been a Piri Indian village long before the invasion of the White man, or go walking in the cottonwood, tamarisk, willow, and Russian olive *bosque* along the Rio Grande. We freaks who lived in La Perla would be running around putting the finishing touches on our contributions to the dinner.

We always invited the old timers who lived in La Perla. Some would come, happy to see the moribund community come to life again, bubbling as it had when they were young. We would take platters of food to others who, because of age and infirmity, were homebound. But there were also old ones who preferred that the town remain comatose and saw the influx of young people as an invasion that was threatening the old way of life when La Perla was a vibrant rural town, the social center of all the little communities for miles around. Ironically, on those days when La Perla was once again the social center, these people stayed inside their houses behind drawn curtains. I think they could not accept that the community they remembered and grew up in was gone and not coming back. But still, for that one day, the entire town was transformed.

On Thanksgiving, the centerpiece of the meal was, of course, the turkey, or more precisely, the turkeys. The cooking of the turkeys was an event in itself. The day before the party, we would dig a pit about four feet square and four feet deep. At sundown, we would light a fire in the pit and keep it burning for hours, building up a thick bed of coals. After the fire had burned out and only the hot coals were left, the turkeys, which had been rubbed with butter and wrapped in layers of wet burlap, would be lowered into the pit directly onto the hot coals. The pit was then covered over by a piece of sheet metal, and dirt piled on it until only a mound could be seen indicating the location of the pit. The turkeys would stay in the pit until dinnertime the next day, when they would ceremoniously be uncovered with all the guests gathered round the pit. By then the turkeys were so moist and tender the meat practically fell off the bones.

After the turkeys were hauled out of the pit and carved, everyone gathered in the yard, usually Louie's, held hands in a serpentine line that wove its way all around the yard, and made a silent prayer of thanks. Then we stuffed ourselves. After dinner there was music and dancing, but most of the guests would be gone by ten that evening.

The Spring Equinox Feast was by far the wilder of the two. Winter, the time of cabin fever and keeping still, was over. Everyone would go crazy and release all their pent up energy. Guests would be arriving all day, and there were expeditions to the *bosque* and the desert, but this feast was primarily a nighttime celebration. We would eat dinner in the late afternoon, usually at Louie's since he had a large, shaded back yard. Then the music would begin. Groups of musicians would play, some inside houses, others outside in the yards, and everyone danced and hollered. There was lots of alcohol and pot as we all celebrated the return of Earth's fertility from its death-like trance. There was a feeling of connection to a distant pagan past, and Dionysius walked once more among us.

One room in Louie's house was set aside for the kids to sleep in as the celebrating went on until the early hours of the morning. Some guests would begin their journeys home at two or three in the morning, but most would find a floor to sleep on in someone's house or roll out sleeping bags outside and stay the night.

The release of tension the Equinox party provided could, of course, threaten to get out of hand. Once, one of the guests, Doug—a huge leather-wearing biker with a reputation for violence— went on a drunken rampage in Louie's house. Shouting hoarsely, he opened the door to the kids' sleeping room and threw an apple into the dark room as hard as he could, instantly drawing the ire of several mothers who closed the door and blockaded it with their bodies. He went into the kitchen where he began kicking and swinging his arms wildly. He literally tore the oven door off Louie's cast iron, kitchen wood stove, and stomped a hole in the wooden floor of the kitchen with his heavy boots. The kitchen was instantly evacuated, and someone went to get Louie, who was neither huge nor violent. Doug stood at six-four and must have weighed at least two hundred and thirty pounds. Louie stood at five-nine and weighed one-hundred-fifty, about one hundred pounds less than Doug. I watched from the kitchen door as they faced each other.

"What are you doing to my kitchen?" Louie shouted.

Doug snarled back—I don't know another way to describe it: He *snarled*.

"Look at what you did to my stove!" yelled Louie as Doug stood there holding a piece of gnawed chicken leg. "This is bullshit!" Louie continued. "You kicked a hole in my floor!"

Suddenly Doug slumped. It was like watching a balloon lose air. He seemed to shrink right in front of us. He set the chicken leg down on the table and stood looking down at the floor, shifting his boot-clad feet. "I'm sorry," he mumbled softly. A minute earlier his voice had been a lion's roar.

"Sorry? I don't give a damn if you're sorry. Who's going to clean this mess and fix my stove and floor? You made a mess of my kitchen and you're sorry. So fucking what?"

For a stunned second I thought Doug was going to cry. "I'm sorry," he repeated, and shuffled out the door. He walked off in the darkness, and the party picked up where it had left off.

I stayed up all night even though the party died around three in the morning. In the grey, pre-dawn light, looking out my window I saw a figure enter Louie's house through the kitchen door. I walked over to see who it was. I peered through the screen door and saw Doug on his knees with wrench in hand as he finished re-attaching the oven door to the stove. When that was done, he began sweeping the kitchen floor. I said nothing and went back to my place. In a short while Doug came out and started cleaning up all the mess in the yard. It took him about an hour and when he was done, he left.

Later I went to Louie's to make coffee for those who had slept on his couch and floor and would soon be awakening. The floor was swept and the dishes washed and sitting in the drainer. There was still a hole in the floor, but what the hell—you can't have everything. The triumph of human decency and civility over the wild savage was more than I could have hoped for. I never saw Doug again. Two weeks later we heard that he had been killed when he crashed his Harley while riding and tripping on LSD.

On one Thanksgiving my friends Kyle and Deborah had brought a friend, Jeni, to the feast. She was the divorced mother of a three-year-old boy. I had met her at the University when we both taught English. I thought her interesting and was attracted to her, but at the same time I found her a bit frightening. She had an intensity and strength of will that made me uneasy. Unlike other visitors to La Perla, she did not talk about how wonderful and meaningful living in our community must be. Instead, she questioned me and what I was doing and why I was doing it. If she noticed any inconsistencies, she pointed them out.

"But you haven't really dropped out. You still use the electricity that is generated by large corporations. Even the running water in your homes is possible because of that electricity. You still have to get jobs and make money. You have cars and use gasoline which some corporation has pumped and refined. It seems to me that what you've done is move out of the city and into the country, but you're still plugged into the system."

Comments like these made me nervous, and I had no real response to them. I might mumble about foolish consistencies being hobgoblins, but her questioning always made me nervous. So even though I felt that she was interested in me, and I was interested in her, I made no overtures to her. Any relationship with her would not be casual, and way down inside me, as much as I disliked admitting it, I knew that I was not capable of such a relationship with another. Not yet. *This is a lady who would give me little leeway*, I thought. *There would not be much wiggle room or maneuvering with her. Everything would have to be straight and straight-forward. I don't want that yet. I'm not ready for that yet. I do not want to be committed to any one person.* So I was friendly, but reserved. Five years down the road, I was ready, and we connected. And we still are.

That Thanksgiving Day I had gone to Tommy's to borrow something I needed for my contribution to the dinner. We were standing outside his house talking when we saw Deborah, Jeni, and their three kids strolling down the dirt road by his house. Tommy stopped talking and looked closely at them.

"Do you know the lady with Deborah?"

"Yeah. I've known her since grad school."

"Does she have a guy?"

"Not that I know of."

"She is one fine lady."

To my surprise I was suddenly upset by his interest in her. I felt *jealous* over a woman I had no claim to nor had made any attempt to get close to. Tommy looked at me intently.

"What about you? Aren't you interested in her?"

"Not that way. She's just a friend."

He laughed. "Just a friend. You better not wait too long. She is a fine lady."

"Wait for what? I told you, she's just a friend."

Annoyed with Tommy, I walked back to my house thinking of what he had said. I realized I was not annoyed because he did not accept my claim of "She's just a friend," but because he had shown an interest in her. I felt he had no right to be interested in her. She was *my* friend. The thought of her with Tommy was upsetting. The thought of her with any man disturbed me. What the hell was going on here? I was afraid to get close to her, was afraid that any relationship with her would involve a commitment and connection I was incapable of. I did not want any relationship that impinged on my solitary "freedom."

The next time I saw Jeni was at the following Spring Equinox Party. She had come down with Kyle and Deborah and the kids again. As usual, the party was pretty wild and Dionysian. One of the guests was Pablo, an older Native American from one of the Indian pueblos that borders the Rio Grande. Pablo dealt in turquoise jewelry, and Jeni admired well-made Native American jewelry. They became close friends, and through her, he had gotten to know many of the freaks. He was considerably older than her, and I was never really sure what their relationship was, rather paternal or amorous, or both. That night, I don't know if he had drunk too much or taken some drug, but he was behaving oddly. I knew him only as a serious and sedate man, but this night he was jumping and hollering along with the young freaks.

During the night, Jeni came and asked me for help. Pablo was harassing her, following her everywhere she went. He would not leave her alone to talk with friends, and later, when she lay down with her son in the room reserved for sleeping kids, he followed her in, kept her son from sleeping, and woke up most of the other sleeping kids.

So I went to Pablo and told him to stay away from her and let her be. He became very angry and hostile, the only time I ever saw him that way. All of his normal courtesy and reserve were gone.

"Who's going to stop me from going to her? You?"

"Yes. She asked me to keep you out of the kids' room, and that's what I mean to do."

He laughed. "We'll see," he said, and went back into the living room to join the dancers.

For the next hour I was constantly aware of where he was, just as he was aware of me. Jeni was still in the room with the kids, getting some rest herself. Soon I became aware that Pablo was no longer dancing, and I went back into the room adjoining the kids' room just as he was opening the door into their room. I pushed him back, closed the door, and stood blocking his path.

"I'm sorry Pablo, but I can't let you in there."

"I can go in there if I want."

"No you can't. Jeni asked me to keep you out, and I'm going to do that."

"Are you her lover, is that what it is?"

"No, I'm her friend, and I'm helping her. You can't go in there."

All the conversations in the room had died, and Pablo and I were the center of everyone's attention. There was a ring of people watching the scene unfold. I guess seeing an Indian wearing moccasins and a red cloth band holding down his hair with its traditional *chongo*—a real, authentic Indian!—threatening a La Perla resident was worth watching. Pablo reached out and grabbed my right shoulder. I was surprised at the strength of his grip, which was making my shoulder throb with pain.

He leaned forward and glared in my eyes. "You don't believe me, but I am a very powerful man. I can do many things to you."

"I believe you, Pablo, but you can't go in this room."

He released my shoulder and stepped back. His eyes were dark and glittering as he stared intently at my face. "By the time the sun comes up, you will be a dead man."

"Maybe, but you still don't go in there."

The room had remained silent through this interaction, almost as if everyone were holding their breath. Pablo turned, pushed his way through the people watching, and walked out. For a moment the room stayed silent, everyone watching me, and then the talking began again, and the event seemed immediately forgotten.

I was nervous for a while—how long was it to sun up?— but gradually the music and joy at the arrival of Spring pushed away my anxiety. The party went on all night, and when the sun came up and I was still on my feet and breathing, I forgot about Pablo's curse. Later, when I saw Pablo getting into his pickup and he wouldn't look at me or say anything, it struck me. That was the first time in my life that I had ever been cursed! A milestone of sorts.

Several friends had breakfast at Louie's, including Jeni and her son. Before she left she apologized for Pablo's behavior and the evening's events, and she thanked me for helping her. I watched her as she got into Kyle's VW bus and continued watching as the bus drove up the mesa and out of sight. I was totally confused about her and the events of the previous day. I went back to my place with Tommy's words echoing in my mind: *You had better not wait too long. She is one fine lady.*

Back in my house, still flush with Spring and the joys of re-birth, I wrote a poem.

>The Spring rains flushed us
>from our holes.
>We rose inquiring,
>eyes glinting in the day
>bright glare of sun.
>The winter sleep was over,
>the sap begun to run.
>
>Frolic on the new-born earth!
>Roll in living mud erotic!
>Ecstatic til the day is done.
>
>That night we sat and chattered
>in our holes
>and talked of greater things to come.

Beyond La Perla

The Great Majestic   Photo courtesy of Bob Christensen

My Life and the Existential Duck Pop

Part of being human is never knowing how much of your feelings and emotions are shared or understood by others, or even if they *can* be shared. Just how cut off are we from one another? Can we bridge the gaps and connect to others? Or are we truly windowless monads, "in the sea of life enlisted?" If you write anything in an attempt to communicate, you are of necessity dealing with that question. The writer must *presume* that he is communicating with the Other. Otherwise, why write? Ultimately writing is an act of faith. *Dammit, I'm going to get through to you if it kills me!* But can I? Really? *Why* I would even want to connect to you is another question entirely.

Let's make the attempt to bridge a gap. Let's see if I can make you understand one of the major turning points of my life. Just for the hell of it.

Sometimes I fall into what I think of as an existential rut. These are times in my life when nothing ever seems to change and nothing that really matters ever happens. Oh, of course things *do* happen: the sun comes up in the morning, I go to work—if I have a job—and I come home in the evening, I eat, the sun goes down, I watch some TV, I go to sleep. The next morning I eat and drink some more. At such times, I am basically a cylinder with a hole for ingesting food at one end, and an anus for evacuating the leftovers at the other. Stasis. Suspension. Entropy. Fear. *Somebody give me something meaningful to do!*

Surely others have felt this way. Maybe not to the depths of despair, maybe you can still navigate through life, but you take no pleasure in just living daily. I can't be the only one who's had to deal with this sort of nothingness. But then that's part of the problem. I really don't know if anyone else has ever felt that way. Reading literature gives me hints that others have felt disassociated from the rest of humanity. "Dotting the shoreless, watery wild/ We mortal millions live alone," writes Matthew Arnold. Or Ishmael. When Ishmael got to feeling restless and useless, he took to the sea, sailing in an ocean of danger, mystery, and fear, where community and cooperation are necessary for survival.

Whenever I got to feeling that way, I would drop everything and run. If I had a car, I drove; if I didn't, I hitchhiked. The important thing was to keep moving, don't stop. As long as I was on the move I had new concerns every day. Where will I sleep tonight? In my car? On the ground by the roadside? How long will my money last? What will I do when I run out of gas or my car breaks down and I no longer have any money? Having to deal with these sorts of problems kept me from thinking about why I was running. And if I ran long enough I could stop, temporarily. That's the problem with running away—whatever relief you get is always temporary.

(You may have noticed a change of verb tense here, from present to past; the feelings I am describing are from years ago. Today if I start feeling disassociated, I no longer have the urge to escape by running. Instead I remember the Great Mysterio and his so-called magic act, Mysterio, who sliced crosswise into my life years ago. Just how many years has it been anyway? Eighteen? Twenty? Not that it makes any difference how long ago it was. I still see Mysterio's performance as the point at which I was forced to face a naked reality that I could no longer run away from.)

Anyway, I can't really say what it was I was trying to run away from. I'm not that precise. I'm not really a thinker in a philosophical or theological sense. My "logic" was, is, a jumble of feelings, emotions, ideas, and imagination. I was incapable of sitting down and examining my life with any objectivity and pinpointing just what it was that made me feel restless and out of place, that *terrified* me, really. I was just carried along with no direction or purpose.

Funny how things happen. You're just cruising along, keeping low, hiding here, there, and then wham! Something, someone, slaps you up alongside the head and sends you spinning, trying to regain what little balance you had. Nothing earth-shaking, nothing you're going to read about in the papers or see on the local evening news, just a grinning clown on the sidewalk who cold cocks you as you walk past. It's of no significance to anyone but you. Nobody else notices, no one else cares but you. Ah, but *you*, you're shaken to your core.

And so it happened. I was in my running away mode, driving aimlessly up and down the West Coast when everything changed. . . .

I'm in San Francisco, on the run again. I can't remember how long I've been running this time. My car is on its last legs, and I am almost out of money and gasoline. I've been renting a room in a cheap hotel for the last few days. I am at the bottom once more, out of a job, almost broke, doing nothing. I'm just hanging, waiting for my car to die so I can have another emergency that forces me to act, to do something, anything. *Only action overcomes fear.*

I'm walking late at night in the Tenderloin District. The fog has rolled in, visibility is at about thirty feet, and the street lights look like miniature stars gone nova. A cold, damp wind blowing in from the ocean knifes through my thin pants, and I walk shivering with my hands jammed into my jacket pockets, my collar turned up. I'm heading back to my cheap room on the third floor of the Sleaze Hotel to see if maybe I can get some sleep. Maybe. I'm slouching past a club of some sort—plate glass window misted over, happy, muffled noises inside—when suddenly the door opens and a man staggers out into the cold. I get a rush of warmth, music, and laughter before the door closes again. I stop. Warm and cozy—just what I need! I open the door and step in.

The club is, of course, small, dark, and smoky, what a promoter would call "intimate." The smell of booze and tobacco permeates the air. An aging stripper is performing an anti-erotic, lifeless routine on a raised platform stage. She is sweating in the glare of an unflattering spotlight. A jazz trio is playing a bump and grind in a corner. The men in the audience are shouting a raucous, laughing commentary on her performance. I go to the bar at the back and order a double shot of bourbon, straight up. I take my drink, find a table and sit down. The light from the spot is filtered through the haze of cigarette smoke, blurring the stripper who seems to be dancing at the bottom of a pool of murky water. Her breasts sag heavily, the lugged out dugs of a tired mom. She seems to be in a trance, oblivious of others' existence.

The jazz combo provides a dramatic flourish, and her dance ends as she strikes a pose, feet apart, one hand on glistening hip, the other held out in front of her as if to keep the crude men around her at a distance. She has a look of pure disdain for them, and for the first time, for one moment, she is truly erotic, the sex goddess not available to those unworthy of her favors. She scoops up the bits of clothing dropped on the floor and disappears through a curtain draped across the back of the stage, accompanied by hoots, jeers, and whistles.

The lights come up and I see an easel, stage left, supporting a blackboard with a notice scrawled in yellow chalk: "Tonite as always! The Great Mysterio and the Existential Duck Pop!" The message is blurred and barely legible.

An emcee, pencil mustache and gleaming slicked-back black hair, bounds onto the stage. "Give it up for the little lady, the exotic Lilah!"

Two or three people applaud, as if under duress.

"And now prepare yourselves for the most astounding magic act ever to appear in The Shattered Egg, nay in the entire state of California! Give it up for the Great Mysterio!"

So now I know the name of the club. The MC leaps off the stage, the drummer does a drum roll, and the Great Mysterio stumbles through the curtain and almost falls on his face. He's dressed in a shabby tux with top hat and black velvet cape, mustache waxed into upward turning points, spotless white gloves holding his gold-tipped wand.

He gestures toward the curtain and says in a whiskey-rasped voice, "Please welcome my assistant, the lovely Lady Mariah!" His lovely assistant steps through the curtain and holds a pose, right hip jutting out, arms above her head, fake blonde hair framing her face. She's too plump and ample for the skimpy, red, rhinestone outfit she wears. Her top threatens to explode out of it. She looks a bit grotesque as she does an ungainly prance around the stage, tottering in spike heels. There is a tear in her black net stocking at the back of her left thigh. The rip is a startling white gash across the dark field of the stocking, like a bolt of lightning in a night sky.

The Great Mysterio works in silence. He bows to his audience and pulls a deck of cards out of his tuxedo pocket with a flourish. He has a bad case of the shakes, and when he tries to fan the cards out, he drops the deck, scattering cards all over the stage. The audience hoots and wails while he and the lovely Lady Mariah get down on hands and knees to gather them up. His lovely assistant then fans the deck and has an audience member pick a card. She holds it up so only the audience can see it. A three of clubs. Coquettishly she slips it into her expansive cleavage. She hands the deck to Mysterio, who fans it out again, has someone else in the audience pick a card, and with a flourish shows it to the audience. We're all expecting to see the three of clubs, but instead it's a jack of diamonds. Mysterio scratches his head bewildered. Lady Mariah excavates within her cleavage, mining unsuccessfully for the card she had stashed somewhere in there.

His act staggers from trick to trick. All of his stunts with cards seem bogus, a parody of the sorts of tricks even a beginning magician does with ease. None of them seem to have a point or purpose. There are no ooohs and aaahs from the audience, only sarcastic hoots and laughter. Another audience member picks a card. Mysterio shows it to the audience, and then cuts it into two pieces. He places the two pieces in his jacket pockets. He then removes his top hat and plunges his hand into it. He feels around with his hand looking more and more confused. Obviously he intended to find the bisected card, made whole again, but instead he pulls out a frilly, purple garter belt. The Lady Mariah quickly grabs it and deposits it in her bottomless cleavage. For an instant I wonder what it must be like when Lady Mariah undresses to go to bed. I have an image of Harpo Marx emptying his coat pockets of silverware, toasters, steam irons, anvils. . . .

All of Mysterio's card tricks lurch along in this inane, pointless way.

Later, Mysterio moves on to more sophisticated tricks, all of which are more than slightly askew. He reaches into his top hat to pull out a rabbit and pulls out a bottle of Jack Daniels instead. When he delicately removes a white scarf out of his lovely assistant's cornucopia of bosom and tosses it into the air, it transforms into a white dove. Obviously confused, the dove flies in circles for a moment, shits on Lady Mariah's head, and then flies into the wall and falls to the floor stunned. The audience is alive and roaring now.

At first I assume his ineptitude is part of the act, and that Mysterio's playing it for laughs, but he seems genuinely flustered and embarrassed. He is not a good enough comedian or actor to pull off such a comic routine. I conclude that he is not a creator of mystery and magic, but merely a clumsy and incompetent trickster.

As the Great Mysterio shambles through the rest of his act, the Lady Mariah takes on a sheen of sweat, and her mascara runs ever so slightly, making her eyes seem like bottomless holes. She is tired now, poor thing; her coquettishness has become strained, and her prancing about has become labored, making her sweat even more.

And then comes the Grand Finale, and it's the Grand Finale that grabs me.

As the final act, his lovely assistant steps forward and hands him a live mallard. Drum roll and a rim shot please! Holding the duck in his left hand, he slips his right hand up the duck's rectum, winding and slithering it along the twisting course of the duck's innards until the hand reappears, jutting from the startled duck's bill. He then grasps the duck's bill and pulls it back sharply—with extreme conviction—pulling the bill back inward, down the duck's gullet, back through its guts until POP! The duck disappears through its own anus. No more duck. Nothing. Nothing at all.

A moment of silence, and then the first applause of his entire act. He bows, and The Great Mysterio and his lovely assistant are gone behind the curtain.

The room remains silent for a few seconds, and then people begin whispering. I sit stunned at what I have just witnessed. I know the duck was there, I know it was real. I saw its heft and solidity as Mysterio held it in his hands. I saw the fear and confusion in the duck's eyes as Mysterio's hand emerged from its bill. An illusion? The Great Mysterio was too much the bumbling fool to pull off any such illusion.

I stumble out into the street in a daze. *Is the duck no more? One puny pop and it's gone? That's it? It's not just the snuffing out of a life; it's a complete denial that such a life ever existed. It's gone forever! How can I know that it was ever really there?*

I head back to the hotel, letting my feet lead me, my mind in such an incoherent jumble that I'm barely conscious of the street. Back in my stale room, unable to sleep, I sit in the darkness. Who is that ludicrous, hopeless "magician"? Why has he affected me so profoundly? Are Mysterio and the Duck Pop emblematic of *my* life, or of life in general? Do we appear on some stage, stumble through roles we're not very good at playing, and then Pop! Off we go, disappearing through our own—or is it God's?— anus. Is that it? Is that all there is?

I sit in the darkness mulling over my life, looking out the window across the street at a red neon sign over a department store, flashing VARIETY, VARIETY, VARIETY, in endless repetition. Nothing in me seems to have a purpose; things just happen randomly, with no plan. Blows come at me from all directions, unanticipated and undeserved. Or so it seems. Is that the way my life is, or is that just the way I've made it?

As the room slowly shifts from black to pale grey, I conclude that I cannot accept that Mysterio's Grand Finale is it, all there is when the curtain drops on the final act. I *refuse* to accept it. No, I am not God's existential duck pop! *My* life will have meaning, even if I have to *force* meaning onto it. It is not a matter of being or nothingness, but a question of attitude. It is *how* I face my life that matters. I will not submit to pointlessness. I know I am a person of no significance in the Great Plan—assuming there is one—just another blip on God's view screen. But maybe with effort I can take something out of my life, something that might be of value to another, or at the very least, make my life intelligible to me.

But what can I do? I've never done anything of any significance with my life. What could I possibly have that would be of use or value to anyone else?

I sit as the sad hotel room comes into detail in the light of the rising sun. I'm not a thinker, a logician. I can't write a treatise explaining why my life should be of any importance to anyone other than myself. And I don't have the faith to believe that there's a god who provides a purpose and meaning for me. I'm not a thinker, but all my life I've learned through my imagination. *Imagination! Stories! Telling stories! Yes, that's it.* I've always told myself stories in an attempt to put sense into the world. *I can create worlds, make order out of chaos!* I even turned my life into a story, the protagonist as observer and participant at once, writing his story as it unfolds.

All stories have an internal logic that orders events. When you begin a story you think you're in charge, you think you know where this story is going to end, but soon the story goes its own way, and you, the maker, must go along with it. Oh sure, I can manipulate the characters and the plot, but only within the limits determined by the characters and the plot. I'm not a thinker, so don't ask me how that works. My life as story is a paradox, the union of control and anarchy.

In a story, fact and fiction become one. Is the tale of Mysterio and the duck pop "true," did it really happen or is it a complete fabrication of my imagination? The question is utterly irrelevant. *It's the story that matters!* I use my imagination to learn about my reality, to try to understand it. In telling the story I have made it part of my life, I have made it "true." Did the event, imaginary or not, really change my perception of life? Obviously it did, or I wouldn't tell it. The story is true; fact and fiction are one.

I shall create my life into a story that is whole and true, weave a robe of coherent design. I may not be a thinker, but I can use my will and imagination to give internal logic and purpose to the story that is my life. Perhaps I can mine my story, using words as my pick and shovel. *To order words and put the world in order!*

I defy the Duck Pop! I refute the purely pointless! I replace the Great Mysterio and his Duck Pop with the Great As-If: I shall live my life as if it mattered, as if it were significant, as if it proved a point, and through my doing so, fiction will become fact.

Hitchhiking

Hitchhiking, a cooperative means of travel, is an ancient and honorable method of transportation which pre-dates the automobile by many years. The word itself comes from the days when horses were the primary means of transportation. If two people on a journey had but one horse, one of them would set out on foot and the other would ride the horse. The one on the horse would soon get far ahead of the one on foot. After an agreed upon length of time or distance, the rider would then get off, hitch the horse to a tree or fence, and set off hiking on foot. When the second traveler got to the horse, he would unhitch it, and ride until he overcame the first traveler and got well ahead of him. Then he would get off the horse, hitch it, and hike. This process of hitching and hiking would be repeated until they reached their destination. This system was good for everyone: The two men had to walk only half the distance to their destination, the horse was not overworked by having to carry two people, and it got to graze while waiting between riders.

The important term here is *horse*. When the horse was the driving power for travelers, people were not insulated from one another as they traveled. If someone on foot or in a wagon or on horseback met someone going the other direction, they would stop and chat. If heading in the same direction, they would chat again, and if one of the travelers was in a horse-drawn wagon and the other on foot, the rider would offer the walker a ride. Travel was a social event.

The automobile changed all that. People in a car are in an enclosed space sealed off from everyone and everything not in that car. They don't want to stop and chat; they don't want to share their space with strangers. For many of them, their car is the only private space they have. When you travel in a car, the world is a high-speed movie you watch through the screen of your windshield. Everything goes whizzing by, including those people standing by the roadside with their thumbs out. They are no longer people but objects in a blurred landscape.

Hitchhiking in the age of the automobile is a much lonelier activity than hitchhiking with a horse. Sure you can hitch rides with a companion, but it is harder for two to get a ride than it is for one. If there are three of you hitching, then the only ride you are likely to get is in the back of a pickup. But in any case, you must have the faith that sooner or later, usually later, someone driving a car will feel an obligation to stop and pick up the wayfarer, for whatever reasons.

During my years as a dropout in social isolation, most of the time I had no vehicle, and I either walked or relied on others for transportation. During this time I literally hitchhiked for thousands of miles, from the deserts of New Mexico to the Pacific coast of California, and from the Mexico border to Canada. Hitchhiking was more than just a means of transportation: It was an adventure and experience that changed the way I move through the world.

When you have to hitchhike in order to get anywhere, the first thing you learn is patience. Nothing happens fast when you hitchhike. As a hitchhiker, you understand that you may likely spend hours sitting by a roadside in all sorts of weather, waiting. And waiting. You learn acceptance. Maybe you've been sitting by the roadside for four hours without anyone slowing down or even acknowledging your existence. You watch the sun dip in the west, and as it gets dark you accept that you are going to spend an uncomfortable night sleeping by the roadside. If that angers or upsets you, then you shouldn't be hitchhiking. Nobody owes you a ride. You must accept that. You must have faith, faith that someone will pick you up, and whoever that someone is will be a person of good will. You are, after all, putting yourself entirely in the hands and care of strangers. You must be willing to accept the opprobrium of people who seem to hate you just *because* you are hitchhiking. I have hitchhiked in the rain sitting by a roadside for hours and had people toot their horns to attract my attention just so they could flip me a finger as they go by. I have been on a lonely desert road and had a car stop fifty yards up the road and wait while I ran toward it, my heavy backpack bouncing clumsily on my back, only to have the car speed off just as I got to it. When you hitchhike you may see people at their worst, but you also see people at their best. And it helps to have a sense of adventure. You never know what's coming when that car slows down and stops in front of you. Hitching a ride was always a trip into the unknown, not always fun or enjoyable, but still an adventure. It is no fun to be dropped off in a residential district of a city when you have no money, do not know anyone in that city, the sun is going down, and you need a place to sleep. So here you are, walking on a sidewalk lined with houses and picket fences, and people staring at you suspiciously through their windows. Where do you sleep then? Hitchhiking often requires you to use your wits.

    I learned that there are certain types of vehicles that almost never pick up a hitchhiker. The driver of a new or recent top-of-the-line car—a Buick, an Oldsmobile, or a Corvette, say—will not even see you standing by the roadside. However, a Buick or Oldsmobile that's ten or fifteen years old with dings and dents, a cracked windshield, and black smoke roiling from its exhaust pipe is a likely candidate to offer you a ride. In the Seventies, any Volkswagen bus splashed with bright colors, decorated with painted flowers, mandalas, or Hindu elephants was a sure bet to pick you up. The poor and other freaks knew what it was like to hitchhike and empathized.

You never know what's coming when a car stops and you open the door and get in. It may be nothing more than a simple, direct, and pleasant ride to your destination, or it may be a doorway into people and places you would never otherwise encounter....

1.

I am walking through Deming, New Mexico with a heavy backpack. I have been on the road for five days, and have no destination. I am just going where my rides take me. A ratty Dodge Dart passes me as I reach the outskirts of Deming and am heading south into the hot, lonely desert toward Mexico. It squeals to a stop. Inside the small car are six people and several bags of groceries. They are from Columbus, New Mexico, about thirty miles away on the Mexico border, and have come to Deming for groceries since there is no supermarket in Columbus. The car's trunk is full of groceries with no room for my backpack, but they manage to squeeze me and my pack into the car. I wind up sitting on someone's knees while another person holds my pack.

"Mom said we were supposed to pick you up," says the young man who is driving.

"There was a voice that told me to pick you up," says a middle-aged woman. "Whenever you hear a voice like that, you gotta obey it."

They are the Hagars, a family from Boise, Idaho, who dropped their middle-class lifestyle after the father died, and like so many others in the Sixties and Seventies, set out on the road in their Dart to look for meaning and purpose in their lives. The oldest, Mark, is twenty-two, Bud is twenty, and Robbie is fourteen. Dale and Ellen, the two others in the car, are friends of the family. They are members of a community outside Columbus, a community they refer to as a "light tower." There are about thirty people renting a cluster of houses. They hold "classes" on the occult, they have séances and communicate with the spirit world, and they do Akashic readings. As I understand it, the "Akashic Records" are the records of everything that has ever happened and will happen, and are stored in some mysterious place not of this earth. An individual, called a "Channel," goes into a trance and recites from the records revealing information about specific individuals or global events.

This group is in Columbus because they are waiting for UFOs from outer space to come pick them up and take them to a better world. The beings in the space ships will separate those who are enlightened, e.g., the people in this community, from the unenlightened, who will be left behind in a sinful, dying world. It is an obvious Star Trek version of the Second Coming of Christ, with Christ replaced by space ships and superior beings from outer space. Evidently there are several of these communities in the U.S. and they communicate with one another.

The Hagars take me in and treat me as one of the family. They expect nothing from me in exchange for the room and board they give me. I live with them for two weeks and attend classes and séances and have an Akashic reading done. The reading is somewhat disturbing. We have just arrived at the Hagars' house after they picked me up when a woman enters the house and announces that she has just received a message that she is supposed to do a reading for someone in the house. Everybody looks at me.

"You're the one," she says.

The next day I go to her house. With three kids in school, she is a housewife, slightly overweight, dressed in a blue shift. There is nothing exotic about her appearance that would indicate her talent as a Channel. She could be any middle class wife/mother. She is in the kitchen preparing dinner when I arrive at the arranged time. We sit at the kitchen table and she tells me to close my eyes and relax, not to think of anything in particular. I sit and in a few minutes the kitchen is drenched in the smell of flowers. There is a vase of flowers on the table which I pick up and hold to my nose. They have scarcely any aroma at all, certainly not the over-whelming odor I am smelling.

"Those aren't the flowers you're smelling, are they?" she asks.

I agree.

"The flowers you are smelling are spirit flowers. I am not receiving anything from you. There is a spirit be-tween you and me, a spirit of someone who recently died, someone you loved very much and is still protective of you. This spirit is blocking communication. Just relax and let the spirit know that you are not in danger or at risk."

I close my eyes and relax. The smell of flowers goes away instantly.

"OK," she says, "the spirit is gone and now I'm get-ting a reading on you. Do you still smell the flowers?"

"No, I don't." What bothers me is that it is now only two months since my oldest brother had died. I was shattered by his death, and my pain and confusion over it were a major reason for my taking this journey, to try to come to terms with his death and my own mortality. I felt that I had to remove myself from my usual friends and activities to put his death and my life in perspective.

"I see you on the roadside," she says while tending a pot on the stove, "wearing a grey hat with a droopy brim, holding a stick in your hand, walking, walking, walking. You have a large pack on your back that bends you over. You are looking for something but you don't know what it is."

Had she seen my hat, I wonder. How did she know about my walking stick which I had to discard when the Ha-gars picked me up? She tells me that when the flying saucers come to sepa-rate the sheep from the goats and take the good folks to a better world, I will help people get on the ships, but I will refuse to leave myself.

"You love the Earth too much to leave," she says, "and you will stay here until it is destroyed and you destroyed with it."

She refers to me as a seeker for truth and tells me that I was guided to this community to help prepare for the arrival of the UFOs and the subsequent departure of the enlightened. I leave her home bemused at the UFO business, and a bit disturbed at her incisive comments about my reasons for being on the road.

When I leave the family after two weeks of their hospitality, we take a group picture with a Polaroid camera. In the picture, everyone is clustered together smiling at the cam-era, except for one dark figure kneeling a few feet to the side, who is obviously not a member of the group. They are sorry to see me go, and I am saddened somewhat to leave them. They are good people, trying their best to come to terms with evil in the world, and trying to live their lives in a meaningful, moral manner. I do not ridicule them, nor laugh at their be-liefs, any more than I would ridicule a Christian and his faith in the Second Coming. As a rule, they are earnest, serious people, honestly concerned with living moral lives.

Without hitchhiking, I would never have known of their world, and their efforts to live meaningful lives. Like so many of my hitchhiking experiences, they expanded my view, made me aware of the manifold ways in which ordinary people try to deal with issues that are not just the abstract concerns of philosophers and theologians.

But there is also a negative side to not knowing who will pick you up, whose control you are going to put yourself under. You often suspend moral judgments on those who pick you up. You're glad just to have a ride, and the space inside the car op-erates on different rules from the world out-side the vehicle. . . .

2.

I have been picked up by people who were obviously on the run from the cops for God knows what crimes, but who treated me decently and kindly. When I leave the group in Columbus, I hitchhike north to Silver City. I am picked up by two men in their late twenties. They are going to Silver City after a night in the whorehouses of Palomas, Mexico, across the border from Columbus. They strike up a conversation with me.

"You know how to get rid of a hickey?" says one who has a red spot on his neck, a memento from one of the whores.

"No."

"You take a pencil and roll it over the hickey." He produces a pencil and rolls it on his neck. The hickey disappears. "Now my girlfriend won't know what I was doing last night." He laughs.

Soon they switch to Spanish and talk about a burglary they're planning, involving a man who has a large coin collection in his house. They are unaware that I speak Spanish. They are fine-tuning their plan when we get to the town of Central, and they turn off the main road. We stop at a bar, and the one in the passenger seat gets out and starts walking through the parking lot, looking into the windows of the vehicles. He stops at one car and motions to us.

"Get out," says the driver.

I comply and follow him to the other car. We get in that car, which has the keys in the ignition, and drive back to the main road. They ask where I want to be dropped off and take me there. I thank them profusely for their kindness. . . .

3.

I was once picked up by a gay man when I was hitching in the rain. He kept trying to seduce me, reaching over while he drove and placing his hand on my crotch.

"I think he's getting hard," he would say.

"I don't think so," I'd respond, making no effort to stop him, even though I have no propensity toward gay sex. I was not eager to go back into the rain.

"Yeah he is, I can feel him stirring."

After extended groping of my privates, he gave up, pulled over at a gas station, and told me the ride was over.

4.

It's ten o'clock in the morning and I am hitchhiking into Albuquerque. A beat-up Chevy Caprice picks me up. The first thing that strikes me as the car jerks back onto the road is the smell—the car smells like a brewery. The two men in the front seat are too drunk to walk, so driving a car is their only option for transportation. As we careen from one lane to another, I think of all the things I never had a chance to do in my life, which I am certain is about to come to an end. At such moments of intense fear your mind can do funny things. I find myself focusing on the Doppler effect as cars heading toward us pass by blowing their horns. Any-thing to allay my fear. In desperation I speak up for the first time.

"Uh, I can get out here."

Both men jump in their seats, looking back at me, startled. I am very aware that the driver is looking back at me while the car goes barreling down the road.

"Who the hell are you?" asks the driver. "What are you doing in my car?"

"You just picked me up hitchhiking."

The two look at each other confused. The car is weaving all over the road.

Thinking quickly I say, "There's a liquor store just up the road if you guys want more beer. I can get out there." I point out the liquor store when we get to it and they pull into the parking lot. I jump out thanking the driver and what-ever entity was watching over me that let me escape alive.

5.

When you sit by the roadside for hours waiting for a ride, or just waiting for any car to come by on a lonely road, hitchhiking becomes a meditation. You have nothing to do but ruminate over your life and how you're living it. You learn that wishing you were somewhere else is futile; you must deal with where you are and forget about wishes. Here and now is where you are, and here and now is where you should be.

When people pick you up, they usually expect you to provide them with whatever they felt was missing when they opted to give you a ride. In a way, they expect you to entertain them, to engage them in conversation that will shorten their journey. This is often the price you pay for the ride, especially with truck drivers in their eighteen-wheelers. Once I was the means by which a driver assuaged his guilt. Nothing about that ride fit the profile: The car was a new Buick with a driver so middle-class he was almost a stereotype in his sharply pressed suit. And he had a handgun nestled be-tween his legs as he drove, a gun which I had not seen until I was seated and the car moving. Otherwise, of course, I would have rejected the ride.

"I often carry large sums of money for my business," he said, looking at me nervously, "and the gun is just for protection."

What on earth made this person decide to pick me up?

"I was driving this road last week," he said. "It was raining and there were a couple of girls hitchhiking, teenagers maybe fourteen, fifteen years old, about the same age as my daughter. I guess I should have picked them up, but you always read about how some guy picks up a hitchhiker and they find the guy later by the roadside dead. I guess I was just scared."

OK. Now I think I know why he is giving me a ride.

His glance toward me seemed to be appealing for my understanding. I was tempted to make the sign of the cross over him and bless him with my forgiveness. Instead I played the role I knew he needed.

"Yeah, you gotta be careful nowadays. Never know what kind of person you're gonna pick up. Hey, I really appreciate your giving me a ride."

He looked at me almost beaming. "Oh sure. Glad to do it."

Tit for tat. I made up for the ride he hadn't given. I realize it took courage for him to overcome his fear and pick me up, and I admire him for it. He must have a strong moral sense, even if it is a cookbook morality—"If you have no mace, you can substitute allspice." It doesn't bother me in the slightest that I have become the means by which he can soothe his conscience. This seems a small price to pay for the ride.

6.

Hitchhiking helped me learn how to connect with people. Throughout this time in my life I rarely read news-papers, watched TV, or listened to the radio. I almost never knew what was going on in other than my immediate world, and so the only topics of conversation available to me were the lives of the people who picked me up.

Once, after a series of mishaps, I found myself in a hitchhiker's worst-case scenario: walking on a lonely, sparsely traveled road in the desert, very late at night. No one is likely to pick you up in those circumstances. The nearest town was forty miles away, it was quite cool and I had no sleeping bag, only the clothes I was wearing. I accepted my situation and concluded that I would spend the whole night walking. To my amazement, after I had walked about an hour a car actually stopped and picked me up even though I did not have my thumb out. It was a man and his fourteen-year-old son. Since I knew nothing of current events, the only subject of conversation available to us was his life and mine. He was returning home from a retirement banquet in his honor. He had been an accountant for a mining company for twenty-five years, and now that he had re-tired, the company had given him a chicken dinner and a watch for his service. He spoke bitterly of having been a cipher in this company for most of his life, of devoting his time and energy for the company, of his wife's running away with another man, leaving him and his son to care for them-selves. While his son slept in the front seat, he questioned me about my life, about my hitchhiking, why I did it, what I expected from life, and whether I thought my life had been a good one.

"You're an educated man," he said after we had talked for a few minutes. "I can tell from the way you talk. Why would an educated person like you be hitchhiking around the country instead of using your education in a career?"

I explained that I had had a career, but once I started questioning what I was doing, I became dissatisfied and dropped out of the mainstream because I needed time to try to sort things out, to think about how I really wanted to live my life.

"Yeah," he said, "I understand that."

When we got to the turn-off to his house, he invited me in for coffee. It was now about two in the morning. He sent his son to bed and we talked until the sun came up. He made breakfast for us and then drove me back to the high-way. When I got out of the car, he thanked me sincerely for having listened to and talked with him. He told me that I, a total stranger, was the only person he had to talk to, and our late-night conversation had helped him accept his situation. Hitchhiking taught me that so many people really have no one to listen to them sympathetically and seriously, and so many of them desire that connection with someone more than just about anything else.

But times have changed. Our reaction to hitchhikers and to hitchhiking is different from what it was in the Sixties and Seventies, and the difference indicates how our society as a whole has changed since that time. There are not nearly as many people on the road as there were then, especially freaks. The pervading attitude toward hitchhikers now is *fear*. Car-jackers, serial killers, rapists—those are the people we assume are hitchhikers today. And this attitude has also affected me. I would never hitchhike today unless it were an emergency. The last time I hitchhiked was when my car broke down on the Interstate and I was riding with my wife and two children. I felt the fear then. I was picked up by a family who stopped only because they saw my stalled car with my family in it. They were kind and generous and drove me to the nearest telephone where I phoned a friend who agreed to come pick us up. The family then drove me back to my car. Today, I wouldn't hitchhike under the same conditions; I would use my cell phone to call a friend and never leave the security of my car.

So even though hitchhiking gave me adventure and knowledge, and taught me lessons which stay with me, the fear that pervades our society keeps me from hitching any-more, and as a general rule, I don't pick up hitchhikers. But every time I drive past a person standing by the roadside, thumb jutting out, I remember the man with the handgun be-tween his legs, and I feel a pang of guilt for letting fear stop me from picking up that hitchhiker, even though hitchhiking is something that has been so important in my life, something which might be equally important in the life of that traveler I just went whizzing by.

Two People on a Journey

by Alex Sanchez

I first met Raf and his friend Jon when I picked them up hitchhiking back in the 1970s. They were headed back to La Perla on Highway 47. We had a very lively conversation (lots of laughs) on the drive down. When we got there, Raf gave me an inside-out tour of one of the restored adobes and I met a few of his friends (some of the characters in his tales I'm sure). I felt welcomed and I was inspired by their efforts to create a real community and revive a dying town. I had seen a similar "resettlement" in northern New Mexico at El Rito. As Raf mentions in *Tales*, this was a pattern repeated in small remote towns throughout New Mexico in the 60s and 70s. After the La Perla and Silver City years, Raf and his family moved to Los Lunas and then Tomé, and we became close friends. We shared many happy times playing volley-ball, tennis, poker and going to social gatherings with friends (the community thing).

Like his award-winning book *The Horse in the Kitchen*, *Tales of La Perla* is an example of Raf's beautiful and direct writing style. Raf had an uncanny ability to tell a seemingly simple story that sticks with you and makes you ponder the deep questions. Raf's journey through life was an adventure of the mind—always questioning, always curious—all in all, a life well-lived. For me, reading these stories feels like sitting under a cottonwood tree (as we did on occasion) listening to him tell a story with that ever-present humorous undertone that reflected his view of the human condition. On a personal level, Raf was my buddy and I miss him greatly.

Bulletin Board

I was managing a bookstore in Silver City and writing poems which I would show to the customers, who would read them and then look at me with a peculiar expression, as if unsure how they were supposed to react. Some would shake their heads bemused, some would smile and say "Nice," and one even said, "I can do that." (He did. He went home and start-ed writing poetry for the first time in his life, which he then showed to me. Not bad.) It was at this time that I got the urge to get a printing press and run my own small publication, featuring area writers and poets. I wanted to publish *real* people's work, none of the scholarly, academic stuff which was read only by other academics, or poetry that was so personal and interior that only the poet and his closest friends could understand it, the "what-I-had-for-breakfast" school of poetry. No, I wanted to print writing that the working, thinking man could gnaw on. So I went to the Green Moon Café and left a notice on the bulletin board that I was looking for a printing press.

    I always used the Green Moon bulletin board when-ever I wanted or needed something that I either couldn't find anywhere or that I couldn't afford to buy. It had never failed me. When I wanted a typewriter, I put a notice on the board, and within a few days someone brought one in and gave it to me, and I set it up on the counter in the bookstore where I wrote my poetry. When I was interested in trying to learn Arabic, someone brought a teach-yourself-Arabic book. Once I deliberately tested the power of the board when I asked for "Dr. Samperson's Electro-Voltaic Belt," an item I had seen advertised in a *Police Gazette* from the nineteen-twenties in the Salvation Army Thrift Store. It was a sort of jock strap, wired so you could run electricity through it while you wore it, and thereby "Increase your virility!" Sure enough, someone brought one in. He had found it in the attic of a house he was renting. I never tried it.

This bulletin board became a source of pride for me. It gave me a sense of power, and I felt as if I were specifically picked by fate for whatever, that there was some force that was watching over me as a special being. I felt I had more control than others over the forces that rule our lives. But this is just the other side of feeling like a victim—both views are false. Anyway, when I wanted to start my own press, one that would eventually and inevitably affect the course of American writing, I put the notice on the bulletin board.

A few days later a dark, burly man with a thick full beard walked into the bookstore. He was about six feet four and must have weighed two-hundred and fifty pounds, a bear of a man. Not, however, a cuddly, teddy bear. This was someone I would not want angry at me.

"Are you the guy that's looking for a printing press?"

"Yeah. You know where I can get one?"

"I'm going to Tucson to pick one up, but I got no place to keep it." He stuck out his hand. "I'm Ray. Ray Luna."

Ray had no literary dreams or ambitions; he was a printer who loved his work and merely wanted to put out his own publication. He didn't care what the publication was. He just wanted to print. We agreed that he would bring the press to the bookstore, and we would keep it in the storage room in back until we could find a permanent place for it.

A week later Ray showed up with a printing press in the back of a pickup. We unloaded it and sat and talked for a long while. Ray had a low, raspy voice which never altered whether he was angry, happy, or frustrated. He talked so softly that I had to listen closely whenever he spoke or I would miss most of what he was saying.

He was a Vietnam vet, supposedly a noncombatant, a finance clerk. It had been his job to make out the payroll for the troops. Once he was sent out in a convoy that went into Cambodia where the U.S. was fighting a "secret war," a spill-over from the Vietnam War.

"Here I was, man, driving a two-and-a-half ton truck through the jungles of Cambodia carrying a safe full of money, looking for combat troops so I could pay them. Jesus, was that looney or what? We got ambushed going through a narrow canyon."

Ray's memory was of total chaos and terror. He talked of the unbelievable din of gunfire and exploding shells, the whine of bullets zipping through the cab of the truck. "I was pushing so hard on the accelerator I thought my foot was going through the floor board. But the damn truck kept moving like a fucking snail.

"I knew I was going to die, man. I knew it as sure as I ever knew anything in my life. Bullets were passing inches from me, and my buddy, Russ—Russell Knowles—was riding shotgun and firing his automatic rifle wildly into the jungle. And all the time we seemed to be going at a walking pace. I was thinking, 'I'm going to die because the god-damned Army wants me to deliver cash to troops fighting in the middle of a goddamned jungle. The fucking Army always pays on time."

And then it was over, as quickly as it had started. Ray was still alive, but his buddy was slumped over the dash board of the truck dead. Ray was splashed with Russ's blood and brains.

"I couldn't believe I was still alive. I was thinking that there must be some reason I was still alive, but I couldn't figure out what it was. Still can't. Why me and not Russ? Sometimes I feel like I was the one that was supposed to be dead, and other times I feel like I can live through anything. But most of the time I feel like I cheated, I got away with something, but now I'm being tracked down and I gotta watch my back all the time. I know I belong to Mr. Bones, and he is gonna come to get his due sooner or later. Fucking Viet Nam, man. Just can't get away from it."

Eventually the convoy found the troops they were looking for, and the Army discharged its financial obligations.

After telling me this tale Ray went to the truck and came back with a saxophone. He sat on a couch in the bookstore, closed his eyes and began playing. He was so big the sax seemed like a toy in his hands, and his thick padded fingers buried the keys beneath them. But he made that sax sing so sweet and mournful my throat balled up. I sat with my eyes closed listening to the music until he stopped, stood up, waved goodbye and left.

Shortly after this the bookstore went belly-up, and we had to find another place to store the printing press. Ray leased a warehouse down by the railroad tracks. It was a much larger space than we needed, but it was cheap. I went and helped him clean up the place. But there was a problem. The previous lessee had left a pile of several tons of bat guano in the center of the warehouse. How the hell were we supposed to clean that?

Ray took his sax and sat on the floor playing. After a while he stopped and said, "I guess I'm in the bat guano business." He silk-screened a bunch of t-shirts with a drawing of a giant marijuana plant and the slogan "Mama Yerba's Bat Guano. Mama knows!" But the guano was not a fast mover, and when he did sell some it was generally a pound or two at a time. At that rate it would take years to clear out the guano. Soon he was unable to pay the rent on the ware-house, so once again we had to move the press. He had a friend in Reserve, the county seat up in Catron County, who had an extra room in his house and had agreed to let Ray store the press there, and even consented to let us print the first issues of our incipient publication out of his home. I helped Ray load the press in the back of his truck.

Ray grinned at me. "Think we can print out of Re-serve? I

bet I can get it set up in two weeks, and if you get the material we can start printing. What shall we call our magazine?"

We discussed various names, most of them humorous or obscene. Then Ray sat on the loading dock playing his sax. I leaned back against the wall, closed my eyes and let the music take me elsewhere, somewhere beautiful and sweet. He stood up. "I guess I can get a hold of you at Edge City?" Edge City, the commune where I lived.

He left for Reserve that evening, carrying the press and our mutual dream. About twenty miles outside of Re-serve, on one of the least traveled roads in New Mexico, he got hit head-on by a drunk driver. The drunk survived, of course, but Ray was splattered all over his truck, and the printing press was a mess of twisted metal.

When I heard the news, I thought of Ray driving through the hell of Cambodia, bullets spattering like rain drops, Ray twisting away from Mr. Bones, delivering cash to fighting, dying troops, and then coming home to respond to an item on a bulletin board in the Green Moon Café, and as a result, dying on a back road in Catron County, New Mexico. And again my throat constricted as I remembered anguish transformed by that sweet, sweet sax. Ray was gone, and with him my desire to start my own magazine.

And I never posted anything on that bulletin board again.

We Actually Called Him Raf
by Betty Mishuk aka Beth

I first met Raf in the mid 70's when he and Jon Jecker, Carol (Bottos) Allen and Carol's toddler Joshua Bottos, came to Silver City to open the New Moon, a little natural foods restaurant and bakery.

It didn't take long before I was lured into their endeavor and became a member of that cooperative effort. Not only did we share the responsibilities of the restaurant and bakery, we lived together, shared vehicles and child care, and together created memories. Silver City in the mid 70's had few alternative lifestyle folks. It was mostly a mining and ranching community. Our presence did not go unnoticed....

One bulletin board posting said, "Wanted, someone to teach me Arabic." That was Raf's. Imagine what attention such a posting might have caused him later. The New Moon is fondly remembered even today in Silver City. It was a place where people came to meet, listen to music, and enjoy a sense of community.

In 1977 Raf, Jon, and I bought a piece of property together that we called "Edge City." It was on the edge of Silver City and we felt like we were on the edge of survival. It had some very rundown buildings on it and a lot of junk. The price was $18,000 and we paid it off at $300/month. We each had our own "bedroom" house and shared a community kitchen and bath. It was a five-acre piece that had been a junk yard for many years, and we proceeded to clean it up. We renovated the buildings. We dabbled in several ventures together from planting large quantities of garlic to worm farming to selling vegetable seedlings. We gardened, planted trees in the neighboring arroyo, and we hauled off junk.

We had goats and chickens. That goat was trouble. Raf lost a borrowed book that he had in his back pocket to that goat. I remember Raf saying, "Free from worry?—Get a goat." Neighbors Skip and Susan Morrison also had a goat, and when the Morrisons needed to be out of town Raf and I would go and milk their goat. Milking the Morrison's goat was a two-person job. The Morrisons kept a broom outside the goat pen and upon arrival Raf would grab the broom, and while I milked he would ward off the Morrisons' attack rooster. Eventually we did get invited over for rooster stew along with anyone who ever had to deal with that mean old rooster. It was tough and stringy and we enjoyed it.

I loved playing scrabble with Raf. We had a running scrabble game going where there was never a winner or loser, just an ongoing score card. He was almost always ahead.

I feel honored to have known and loved Raf. He was a kind and gentle soul. I loved his wit and humor. He will always remain special to me. Because of Raf I now am blessed with Geri in my life.

Editor's Note: Betty still lives in Silver City. She plays "Words with Friends" now and beat me so often I finally gave up. That didn't stop me from lightly editing this piece she read at Ralph's Memorial in September 2017.

Firewood Run

I awake in the cold darkness well before dawn. I know I should get up and light a fire in the kitchen stove, but it's so cold I just lie nested in my bed warmth, sleepily feeling my energy drift away. Then I remember the wood run; today we must replenish our wood supply, so even though it is not a workday at the Green Moon Café, everyone will be up early. If I want time to myself I have to get up quickly, before peo-ple start coming over for breakfast.

I slip shivering into my heavy wool robe and slip-pers. Moving jerkily in the cold like a puppet, I go to the cast iron kitchen stove and clean out the ashes in the firebox from last night's fire. I then ball up pages from the *Albuquerque Journal*, stuff them in the firebox, add some kindling, and light the paper. I open the side vent on the firebox, close the oven flue, and open the damper on the stove pipe. I wait a moment while the kindling crackles, then add larger pieces of wood—juniper at first, since the fire is not yet hot enough for oak. Soon the fire is roaring, so I close down the damper and put some water on for coffee. Now I can add some oak to the flames. My breath is no longer visible.

I wash up in the bathroom with frigid water and then head back to the stove to warm up. There is no sign of light in the east yet, so I sit in the rocker next to the stove and read *The Iliad*, waiting for the coffee to brew. Just me, Achilles, and Hektor. Slowly the eastern sky begins to lighten.

Joel comes in. He's upset about something and does not respond to my greeting. He walks directly to the stove and hurriedly begins making his breakfast. Chi comes in a few minutes later, mumbles a cheerless greeting to no one in particular and proceeds to make his breakfast. Joyce comes in with her two kids. She's short-tempered and snaps at them. In a minute Joel is telling the kids to be quiet or go outside in the cold. Everyone eats quickly and quietly. I pull inward and go back to *The Iliad*.

After breakfast there's a rush to get everything ready for the wood run. Plywood side-extenders have to be bolted to the sides of the trucks to allow for larger loads. Food has to be packed, tools gathered. Everyone goes outside to get the trucks and equipment ready, but I stay inside to make lunches since I don't want to be around the others when they are so tense.

Bob, who lives in Silver City, has spent the night at Edge City because he wants to help gather firewood. He and Beth come in together.

"What's everybody so pissed off about?" asks Beth.

"I dunno. Nobody's talking."

I immerse myself in the food packing, making sure all the thermoses are filled with coffee, lots of coffee, and the water containers are filled. I pack fried chicken, cheese, bread, cookies and fruit. I then go outside and help gather tools: axes, saws, wedges, sledge hammer, maul, and a shovel in case we get stuck in sand and have to dig our way out. I load everything in T.G. Scott, our 1950 Dodge one-ton stake-bed truck. Joel and Chi are bolting the plywood side-extenders onto T.G. No one is speaking. I go back into Main House and wait.

By eight o'clock everything is ready. We drive our two trucks to Silver City to meet up with Ben and his two sons and their truck. They don't need firewood but are going along to help. From there we head toward the Big Burro Mountains in the Gila Forest, southwest of Silver City. Joel, Bob, and I are riding in T.G. Scott with the two other trucks following. Slowly the houses are left behind, and the wind-mills and stock-watering tanks begin.

The sun is shining bright and the air is warming. Bob chuckles and points a finger at Joel.

"You may be disgruntled, but I'm delighted to be going on a wood run."

Joel does not respond.

We climb slowly, past the Tyrone Mine and into the Gila Forest. In the cab Bob and I exclaim over the beauty of the forest morning and begin making small talk. Gradually Joel joins in.

Some twenty miles outside of Silver City we get to the site of the Macomas Massacre Historical Marker, evidently commemorating the massacre of some folks by other folks back in the day. We leave the highway and get on to Gold Gulch Road, a sandy forest service road that runs along the bottom of a dry wash. We move slowly through the forest, worried about getting stuck in sand and watching for dead wood. At a junction with another service road we stop and hold a conference with the others. We decide to separate and reconvene there after all trucks are fully loaded. Joel, Bob, and I continue in T.G., winding through deep, treacherous sand, five miles an hour up a dry wash. After half an hour the road levels off and becomes hard-packed. We spot sev-eral dead oaks. We stop and clamber out. We will have to haul the wood about fifty yards to the truck.

It's warm and clear now. We strip off jackets and sweaters, grab saws and axes, and move up the slope to the dead wood. The oak is hard to cut and heavy to haul, but soon my muscles loosen, become lithe and supple as I fall into the rhythm of my saw. Sweat runs down my face and into my eyes. A short distance away I hear Bob singing plaintively:

> *Lord I'd rather drink muddy water,*
> *Sleep in a hollow log;*
> *Rather drink muddy water,*
> *Sleep in a hollow log,*
> *Than to be in some dark city*
> *Being treated like a dirty dog.*

The oak, juniper, and ponderosa pine—tall and green, the range grass gold and rustling, the air saturated with the taste of tree and mountain, the sky blue and endless. They are here, they have always been here, and they will live for-ever in my memory. My temporality vanishes and I become immortal. My mind jumps and spins in joy.

But the wood must be cut and hauled. The singing ceases and all energy is directed toward wood gathering. I take a large section of oak, maybe seventy-five pounds, and grunting maneuver it onto my shoulders and begin the long, unsteady walk down to the truck where Joel is using a chain-saw to cut the large sections into eighteen-inch rounds to load in the truck. The rounds will be split after we get the wood back to Edge City.

The work continues all morning and well into the afternoon. Each log gets heavier and heavier. After hauling a log to the truck I must lean against the fender until I catch my breath. Then back up the slope for more wood. We take turns hauling logs, oak and juniper, and cutting rounds. By the time we have a full load, each breath I draw is painful, my arms are leaden, and I am dizzy from exhaustion and hunger.

With a full truck we drive back to the rendezvous point. Ben and his boys are there with a full truckload. We sprawl on the ground until Joyce and Chi show up with an-other truckload. Ben has brought a bottle of wine to go with lunch. We devour lunch in silence, and then lie back and look at the clouds scudding across the sky. No one talks but it is a silence of fulfillment, totally different from the tense silence of the morning. After an hour we mount the trucks and begin the slow trip back home. The air is chill as the sun droops and the shadows lengthen.

Back on the highway, just before sunset, coming over a rise I notice a black dog by the roadside at the bottom of the rise, several hundred yards away. As we approach, the dog becomes a spirit dog, changes shape, becomes magical, gro-tesque, and then it leaps into the air and crosses the road in front of us, a few feet above the pavement. It turns and moves parallel to the road, coming toward us, and as we go by each other I see through the window the curved beak, the fierce eyes, and the huge, swooping wings.

"Jesus!" says Joel. Then all three of us together: "An eagle!"

The truck behind us is tooting its horn. I lean out the window and look back. Joyce is sticking her head out the window and waving in the direction of the now disappeared eagle. I wave back and we toot our horn excitedly....

It is dark when we get back to Edge City. My glasses fog up the instant I enter Main House. The air is rich with the smell of cooking beans and freshly made tortillas, and two pumpkin pies that Beth has baked while we were gone. The kids have stayed home with Beth and are squealing, jumping, hugging in joy at our return.

"Oh no," says Beth after everyone has calmed down. "I forgot to milk the goat. Would somebody keep on eye on this tortilla while I go do that?"

Joel nods assent, and Beth puts on her jacket and goes out to milk Goatee. I sit, bone-weary, looking out the window at T.G. Scott's silhouette. I can see the outline of the firewood piled high above the cab. Life is good.

Tomorrow, tomorrow will be a good day for splitting firewood.

T.G. Scott   Photo courtesy of Betty Mishuk

The Iliad at 4 a.m.

In my nineteenth year
I read *the Iliad*
and dreamed I was Achilles
hidden in my tent
listening to the sough and rustle
of the brooding sea,
waiting for my destiny
to bring me death
and immortality:
Troy destroyed and Greece emerging
through my strength and sacrifice.
Now at forty-eight
I huddle by my winter fire
reading Homer once again.
I am Hector
backed against the bolted gates;
across the plain Achilles comes
mighty in his rage.

Zeus tips the scale.
From the wall above,
a keening wail.

Lunch beneath the Bo Tree

For a while I worked in construction with a—dishonest, as I discovered later—local contractor. He specialized in expen-sive adobe houses. I worked for him making adobe bricks, loading and unloading adobes, and mixing and hauling ce-ment for mortar. Chuey was my mentor on the crew.

Chuey was an *adobero*, someone who mixes up a pit of mud, shovels the mud into wooden forms to make sun-dried adobe bricks, and then builds houses out of them. For a while I was his *aprendiz*, his apprentice, and he taught me how to make good adobes, how to toss and load adobes onto a flatbed truck, unload and stack them at the building site, and mix up the mortar to bind them together and transform them into a house. The process seems almost magical: from common dirt to beautiful home.

Like everything important in life, tossing adobes re-quires a developed skill. Each adobe weighs about thirty-five pounds, and there are often jagged pebbles and shards of glass embedded in them. Once removed from the forms and sun-dried, hundreds of them must be moved onto the back of a truck, and then driven to the job site, where they are unloaded. Thirty-five pounds apiece. To load and unload, the workers form a line, each person about ten feet apart. When you toss an adobe it must make one-half a revolution before it gets to the catcher, so that what was the bottom when you tossed it is now the top. It should get to the catcher precisely at waist level and not be spinning when it arrives. The catch-er cradles it as it arrives—35 pounds!—as gently as if he were catching a baby tossed out the window of a burning building. In one fluid movement he turns as he catches it and tosses it to the next man in the line. If you don't do it this way bad things can happen. The catcher may wind up trying to catch a whirling 35 pound block, and at the end of the day he will for sure have battered hands if not a broken toe from a dropped brick. A dropped brick is a broken brick, and eve-ry broken brick is wasted time, effort, and money.

Chuey showed me the natural beauty of adobe, how a house made from soil rises from the soil and remains a house as long as people live in it and care for it, but when they leave and the house is abandoned, how the mud bricks dissolve and the house returns to the soil from which it sprang. Eventually there is only a low mound where the house once stood, a mound covered by cactus, weeds, wild-flowers, and an occasional man-made arti-fact—a broken mir-ror or a hairbrush or pencil stub—to show that folks once lived here, beneath the mound.

"This is the way it should be," Chuey said. "Houses are like bodies: When they die they should go back to where they started, here"—at this point digging the heel of his boot into the ground. "That way they can be used again, to make more adobe or to feed some plants."

Chuey was short and squat, about five feet five, and one hun-dred seventy pounds. His head was as bald as a white bowl-ing ball, and about the same size, and when he laughed—which was often—he looked like one of those stat-ues of the laughing Buddha, eyes squinting in laughter, hands resting on his pro-truding belly. His forearms looked like they had quarter-inch cables buried under the skin. When you catch and toss thirty-five-pound adobe bricks as a regu-lar part of your job, loading a flatbed truck with thousands of bricks and then unloading them at the building site, your arms and shoulders get quite a workout. When I worked in adobe I was in the best physical condition of my life. Chuey was fifty-two, but whenever it came to hard work, I would pit him against any man half his age.

Chuey was the first native-born and U.S. raised American I ever knew who was completely illiterate. Raised on the U.S. side of the border with Mexico, in Texas and New Mexico, Chuey was more at ease speaking Spanish than English. In fact, he spoke English only when he had no choice. Only once in his life had he been farther south into Mexico than the border-town whorehouses, yet he was with-out question much more Mexican than American.

One day, lying in the shade of a cottonwood at noon, resting our tired bodies and eating our lunches, he told me about his life.

"In the state pen," he told me in Spanish, "they taught me three things: to keep my mouth shut, to do leather work, and to write my name. The first of these was the most im-portant thing I learned there."

"Why were you in the pen?"

"Because I was stupid. Me and a friend, equally stu-pid, held up a liquor store in Las Cruces. The store owner got our license number before we drove away, and we got arrested the same day. I did three years." He shrugged. "I did not like being locked up, so I never did anything like that again."

His father had been a soldier in the Mexican Revolu-tion of 1910, but on whose side was never clear. As the fighting in Mexico ground to an exhausted halt, Chuey's dad was shot by agents of the government who were seeking to arrest him for unspecified crimes against the Revolution. Although wounded he managed to escape them, and his brother smuggled him across the Rio Grande from Ojinaga, Mexico to Presidio, Texas. In Presidio he recuperated from his wounds and acquired a Mexican-American girlfriend. In Mexico there was a price on his head. This was in 1919.

Soon the ex-Revolutionary and his woman moved from Presidio to Corona, New Mexico, where he hired on as a ranch hand. But trouble followed Chuey's father wherever he went. He was a violent man, very quick-tempered, and he always carried a gun—a bad combination. In Corona he got into an argument with someone in a bar, and shot and killed him. When a deputy came to his house to arrest him, he shot and wounded the deputy.

He escaped across the border and returned to Ojinaga, which was once again safe for him since the post-Revolution government had granted amnesty to revolutionaries who had been accused of crimes. He sent word to his wife and two kids in Corona to return to Presidio, Texas where his family moved in with his wife's parents while he stayed in Mexico. Every night he would sneak across the Rio Grande and "co-habit" with his wife in Presidio. Every morning, before sun-rise, he would return to Mexico. In this manner were Chuey and two sisters conceived.

When Chuey was about eight years old, his dad heard that the trouble in Corona had blown over somehow, and he could probably return and not be arrested. So he sneaked across the border one more time, changed his name, and took his family and moved back to Corona, where once again he took a job as a ranch hand. The family settled into respecta-ble poverty.

After a few years, Chuey's dad and his uncle, his mom's brother, decided to open up a Mexican food restau-rant in Corona. Shortly after the business opened, the two partners got into an argument over a business matter. Chuey's uncle accused his dad of taking money from the till.

"He probably did take the money since he was not too strong on morals, and he had been a thief before, but he was a man of honor and would let no one *accuse* him of being a thief. Well, I told you he always carried a gun, so he drew it and shot and killed his brother-in-law. He ran back to Mexico where he lived the rest of his life. I was twelve years old, and I never saw him again."

For years afterwards, at irregular intervals from un-expected sources, Chuey would hear bits of gossip and ru-mors about his father in Mexico. What he heard was never good: robbery, cattle rustling—trouble just seemed to follow his dad everywhere. He never heard anything from his father himself.

One day, when Chuey was a full-grown man, he heard from a Mexican relative that his father was very ill, possibly dying, in a small village in the hills of Chihuahua. Chuey hurried into Mexico in hopes of seeing his progenitor before he died. He got to the village just as they were packing the dirt over his father's grave. This was the only time Chuey had ever gone farther south than the border towns. His father had died that morning, and since no one knew the whereabouts or names of any relatives, they buried him that same day.

And so, thirty years later Chuey was telling me this story in the shade of a cottonwood at a job site. He finished his tale then lay back and stared at the summer sky for a while. Then he sat up.

"You know, I don't think anything happens to people when they die. I've seen guys die—I've seen them stabbed and shot—and at first they're in agony, but when they know they're dying for certain, it's like all the pain and suffering stops, and they just die without fighting it. You look at them and you know it's all over for them—no more pain, no more suffering. It's *living* that's the pain and suffering, not dying. I just can't believe that God punishes people for things they have to do in this life. I mean, I believe in God, *mi tata Dios*, but you know, sometimes a guy has to do all sorts of bad things just to stay alive, things he may not want to do but he doesn't have a choice. I think God understands that, and He kinda looks away when you gotta do something that's maybe not too good. He knows you gotta eat, your family's gotta eat, and nobody helps poor people. Sooner or later, every-body's gotta do stuff they're not proud of. Isn't that what living is like?"

I found myself assenting reluctantly.

He lay back, silent again. Then he sat up with a loud whoop.

"*Chingado!* My father spent his whole life fighting and on the run and died alone in some stinking little village. Me, I work and sweat until even my hair aches, and I never have enough money to pay all my bills and buy stuff for my kids. I work like a *burro!* Every day it's *tras, tras, tras,* with no relief, and I never get ahead. This damned life! But you know what? I would rather be alive and suffering in this life than dead and at peace. Aint that the craziest thing you ever heard? Aint that the goddamndest thing you ever heard?"

He leaned back against the tree and laughed and laughed, his hands resting on his rotund belly.

Old adobe under trees   Photo by Geri Rhodes

Rocks

My wife and I live in a small, lovely rural community in the central Rio Grande Valley of New Mexico. Our home is bounded on three sides by fields of alfalfa and pasture grass. On the west side, our property abuts an irrigation ditch about fifteen feet wide with a ditch road on either side. The ditch roads are not public thoroughfares; they are maintained by the Rio Grande Conservancy, a state agency, for the use of the ditch rider who is responsible for delivering the irrigation water on schedule to local farmers and seeing that the ditches are clear and maintained. Vehicle traffic on the ditch roads is rare. In summer, one of my wife's and my daily rituals is to take a walk along the ditch road with our dog Isis. (I would never name a pet after any deity, but the dog was a giveaway and came with the name. I must say, however, she has never done anything to dishonor the name.) This walk is the high point of my dog's day.

Isis can go for a walk in the countryside pretty much whenever she wants, but she never does unless my wife and I, or either one of us, goes with her. It isn't *the walk* that matters; it's *sharing* the experience she loves with those she loves that is important. When we go, her joy and excitement are contagious. She struts and bounces, runs back and forth along the road, wanders into the farm fields and rolls gloriously in the greenery and livestock manure.

For a long time I was bemused by her excitement. After all, the walk never changes; it is always the same walk. The only difference is whether we choose to go north or south on our jaunts along the ditch. We always stop at the same points in the road where we turn and walk back home. But for her, it is obvious that one day's walk is completely different from the previous day's journey. There are not many people who walk on the road, but there is an abundant wildlife. Every morning there are fresh tracks in the road: raccoons, skunks, coyotes, dogs, and other unidentified spoor. She sniffs every track of every critter that walked that road during the previous night, as if trying to reconstruct the nature of the travelers and the order in which they walked the road. Other times she will pause and stand still with her muzzle pointed in the breeze toward the direction of a new smell emanating from a distant source. At such times she glances at me as if to ask, "Did you get a whiff of that?!" I, of course, smell nothing. Literally nothing. I ignore even the smells immediately around me, the ditch water, the flowers, the newly mown alfalfa. For me, same road, same walk, nothing new. So she stops to smell and I keep going.

I'm sure she must think I am somewhat mentally underdeveloped. I seem to miss everything going on around us in the world. So I have started stopping when she stops, and I point my attenuated muzzle in the direction she is looking, as if I too were picking up the same scent. After all, I don't want my dog to think poorly of me. I try hard to be the person she thinks I am.

I know the differences between us are rooted in the different strengths of our respective senses. Her sense of smell is incomparably more powerful than mine and her hearing is much more acute. But our walks have made me aware that it isn't only a matter of the relative strengths of our senses that makes her more aware of what's going on around us. It is ultimately a question of *ignorance*. Whereas I *ignore* much of the world around me— nothing new, same old, same old—she pays attention to every detail. New adventures may come at any time. For me, distinctions blur in my world of weak focus. But she has been a good teacher. I have gradually learned to pay attention too, and I have found much beauty in the manifold daily details of the world around me.

Last summer I wanted to put some rock borders around the shrubs and flowers by our front door, so I picked up at least one rock every time I went on a walk with Isis. At first they were nothing special, just rocks. But then I started looking at the rocks closely, noting distinctions among them—shapes, sizes, colors, textures, all unique, all different. So I started choosing rocks carefully, picking this one and rejecting that one on the basis of a purely subjective response. At first I felt foolish and embarrassed. Here I was, reverting to childhood, playing with pretty pebbles, but then I began to understand that we *must* become more childlike to regain some of the wonder and excitement over the world that we felt as children, and which Isis feels now.

So I picked rocks carefully, holding each one in my hand, feeling its heft and texture, looking closely at shades of color, patterns, intricate designs, getting deeper into aspects of the world I had been ignoring since I left childhood. (Yes, children do pay more attention to "insignificant" details). I took each rock home, and picked the exact spot I wanted to put it, integrating it with the rocks I had already brought. At first I thought my wife must think I had fallen off the edge, but she too became involved with our rock gathering. Though I was certain no one would ever see the same beauty and design that I saw in our rock borders, that simply made no difference. I saw it, and that meant my perceptions had changed, and changed for the better.

I was right; nobody ever noticed the rocks. Nobody, that is, until Carlo, a young man who lives up the road a short ways, came to visit. As he approached my front door, he stopped at the rocks I had placed around the Russian sage, knelt down, and picked some up, looked at them intently, and then replaced them carefully back in the exact spots from where he got them. We said nothing, but there was an instant bond. We knew that we both understood about the rocks and their inherent beauty.

But Carlo is hardly your typical young man. Shortly after he noticed our rocks, he gave my wife and me a hefty rock that must weigh over a hundred pounds for our anniversary. He had come across it on one of his walks in the desert, marked its location, and drove out in his pickup and brought it home. He decided to honor my wife and me by giving it to us. I am not being sarcastic or facetious when I say "honor." The three of us looked around our yard and carefully picked the exact spot to place the rock. Now when I am working in my yard I often stop and *look at* the rock. There is always something new to see, some minuscule pattern in a world within a world.

But no one else notices our rocks. No one has ever asked about the huge, lone rock sitting in the middle of our yard. No one looks at the rocks bordering our shrubs and flowers. Perhaps they simply don't see them. Why should they? They're only rocks.

Carlo's Rock   Photo by Geri Rhodes

Afterword

by B.G. Burr

I can't remember when I first met Raf. Sometimes it seems like I have always known him, know everything about him and his journey through life. Sometimes it seems like I just met him and don't know anything about him. That might be strange since I played poker with Raf nearly every Friday night for the last forty years. When you play poker with someone that often you can usually figure out their "tells", those involuntary tics and telltale expressions that let you know whether they have a really good hand or are just bluffing. In all of that time playing poker with Raf, I never figured out a single tell. I never knew if he had a flush or a nine high hand. His smile was always the same, amused but inscrutable.

He had me figured out, though. When his book, *The Horse in the Kitchen*, was published by UNM Press I asked him to inscribe my copy to my wife, Laura, and me. It was pure Raf that I had to first buy the book. He gladly obliged, and quickly wrote something on the title page. He closed the book and handed it back to me. For some reason I didn't want to read it in his presence, so I just took the book and tucked it away to read the inscription later. At the first opportunity I opened the book and read: "To B.G. and Laura. Two dear friends and one mediocre poker player."

Though unspoken, I always wanted Raf's approval. I wanted him to think I was as clever and knowledgeable as I knew he was. I never found out what he thought. He died before I had a chance to ask him about it, or he had a chance to say anything to me. Not that I would have asked or he would have said anything anyway. He didn't invite that sort of intimacy.

That's why I have enjoyed this book so much. Raf expresses ideas and emotions here that he never shared with me. To me, it represents a last, sweet gift of his inner self that I didn't have access to otherwise. I wish I could thank him for that gift. But I can't. He's gone. Too soon, and I miss him more than I can say.

Raf at B.G.'s   Photo courtesy of B.G. Burr

NOTES

www.ingramcontent.com/pod-product-compliance
Lightning Source LLC
Chambersburg PA
CBHW051648040426
42446CB00009B/1034